Making t
To Pc

Lucia Langston
Copyright © 2023

All rights reserved.

ISBN: 9798397610254

DEDICATION

Dedicated to the ones who dare to dream of an extraordinary life. The seekers, the adventurers and the believers that there's "more" to life. You've heard the whispers of possibility, you've felt the stirring in your heart. This is for you.

CONTENTS

ACKNOWLEDGMENTS

I am deeply grateful to the warm, hospitable and beautiful people of Portugal. Their kindness, spirit and way of life have taught me so much about being present in the moment and living joy. Obrigada for making this experience unforgettable in so many surprising and wonderful ways.

INTRODUCTION

Olá! Bem-vindo!

Hello and welcome. So you're thinking of relocating to Portugal? I'm glad you're here and to be your guide. Let's look at your path to Portugal.

Embarking on a journey that takes you far from the familiar and towards the unknown, can be both exhilarating and daunting. Moving to a new country is an experience that holds adventure and possibilities. A chance to reinvent your lifestyle, immerse yourself in a vibrant culture, and embrace variety. That is the spice of life after all.

Portugal has emerged as the destination of choice for individuals seeking a change of scenery and more chilled pace of life. Whether you're contemplating a move from the United Kingdom, United States or any other English speaking country, this book serves as your comprehensive guide in making the move the Portugal and beyond.

Within these pages, we'll navigate the intricate process of moving to Portugal, from the initial spark of inspiration to the moment you step foot this Eastern corner of Europe. With its stunning coastline, rich history, and warm Mediterranean climate, Portugal has captured the hearts of countless expatriates seeking a slice of paradise. Maybe you're enticed by the golden shores of the Algarve, the alluring city life of Lisbon, or the tranquil charm of Porto, Portugal offers a diverse array of experiences whatever your desires.

As someone who's lived in six countries I can vouch that moving to a new country demands careful planning and consideration. In this book, we'll provide you with all the essential information you need to know about visas, residency permits, and the legal requirements for establishing a new life in Portugal. From navigating the bureaucracy to understanding the intricacies of healthcare and taxation systems, we'll demystify the logistical aspects, ensuring a smooth transition for you and your loved ones.

But relocating to Portugal is not merely about navigating paperwork and logistics; it's a transformative journey that encompasses much more. We'll delve into the cultural nuances, offering insights into the Portuguese way of life, customs, traditions, and social etiquette. Understanding the local language, learning about the culinary delights, and immersing yourself in the vibrant local communities will enrich your experience and foster a sense of belonging.

We'll explore the various regions of Portugal, highlighting their unique features and characteristics. From the sun-soaked beaches of the Alentejo to the enchanting vineyards of the Douro Valley, Portugal offers a wealth of breathtaking landscapes and hidden gems waiting to be discovered. We'll guide you through the process of finding accommodation, choosing the right neighbourhood, and embracing the lifestyle that aligns with your dreams and aspirations.

Through firsthand accounts, practical tips, and expert advice, this book aims to equip you with the knowledge and confidence to embark on this life-changing adventure. Whether you're seeking to retire in the tranquil Portuguese countryside, start a business in the bustling capital, or simply immerse yourself in a rich tapestry of history and culture, Portugal is a welcoming and wonderful choice.

So, let's explore the path that leads from the United Kingdom, USA or other parts of the English speaking world outside the EU, to the sun-kissed shores of Portugal. Let this book be your compass, your guide and equip you with the tools to make the most of your new life.

The wonders of Portugal await you, and the possibilities are endless.

From Dream to Reality
Let's take a tour of what we're going to cover in this book.

Chapter 1: Discovering Portugal's Allure

1.1 Unveiling the Magic: Why Portugal?

Portugal's allure captivates the imagination of many, drawing people from all corners of the globe to its shores. In this section, we'll delve into the myriad of reasons why Portugal has become an irresistible destination for those seeking a fresh start.

1.2 The Joys of the Portuguese Lifestyle

Immerse yourself in the Portuguese way of life, explore the unique cultural aspects and daily rhythms that make this country so special. From the warm hospitality of its people to the slow-chilled afternoons, uncover the essence of the Portuguese lifestyle.

1.3 The Great Escape: Seeking an elevated Quality of Life

Discover why Portugal consistently ranks highly in global quality of life indexes. We'll examine the factors that contribute to the country's exceptional healthcare system, safety, and overall well-being, ensuring you understand the benefits that await you in your new home.

Chapter 2: Preparing for the Journey Ahead

2.1 Assessing Your Motivations: Defining Your Purpose

Before embarking on this life-altering journey, it's essential to reflect on your motivations for moving to Portugal. In this section, we'll help you articulate your goals, whether it's a change of scenery, career opportunities, or a desire for a slower pace of life.

2.2 Researching and Selecting Your Destination

Portugal boasts a diverse range of regions, each with its own distinct character. We'll guide you through the process of researching and selecting the perfect destination that aligns with your preferences and aspirations, whether it's the vibrant city life of Lisbon, the tranquil coastal towns of the Algarve, or the cultural heritage of Porto.

2.3 Financial Considerations and Budgeting

Moving abroad entails financial planning and budgeting to ensure a smooth transition. We'll discuss important aspects such as cost of living, taxation, healthcare expenses, and other financial considerations you need to account for when moving to Portugal.

Chapter 3: Navigating the Legal Landscape

3.1 Visa and Residency Options

Understanding the visa and residency requirements is crucial to ensure a legal and hassle-free relocation. We'll provide an overview of the various visa options available, including the Non-Habitual Resident (NHR) tax regime, the "Golden Visa program", and the residence permit application process.

3.2 Navigating Bureaucracy: Essential Documents and Procedures

Dealing with administrative processes can be overwhelming, but fear not, as we'll guide you through the necessary paperwork, including obtaining a Portuguese Tax Identification Number (NIF), opening a bank account, and registering with local authorities.

3.3 Healthcare and Insurance

Maintaining good health is a priority when moving to a new country. We'll explore the Portuguese healthcare system, outline the options for private health insurance, and help you understand how to access quality healthcare services in your new home.

Chapter 4: Making the Move

4.1 Packing and Logistics: What to Bring and What to Leave Behind

Deciding what to pack and what to leave behind can be a challenging task. We'll offer practical tips on minimising the stress of moving your belongings, including suggestions for shipping, storage, and dealing with customs regulations.

4.2 Finding Accommodation: Renting, Buying, and Temporary Stays

Securing suitable accommodation is vital for a smooth transition. We'll provide insights into Portugal's rental and real estate markets, help you navigate the process of renting or buying a property, and explore temporary housing options for your arrival.

4.3 Settling In: Establishing Networks and Connecting with the Community

Building a support network and integrating into the local community is essential for a successful transition. In this section, we'll guide you on how to establish networks, connect with like-minded individuals, and immerse yourself in the vibrant Portuguese community. From language learning resources to joining local clubs and organisations, we'll help you find your place in this new chapter of your life.

Chapter 5: Your New Life in Portugal

Congratulations! You have made it to chapter five where we will dive into the exciting realm of building your new life in Portugal. By now, you have navigated the intricate process of moving to this captivating country, from the initial spark of inspiration to the moment you set foot on its shores. In this section, we will provide you with valuable insights, practical tips, and essential information to help you settle in, integrate into the community, and embrace the Portuguese way of life.

5.1 Embracing the Culture and Lifestyle:

One of the most fulfilling aspects of moving to a new country is immersing yourself in its unique culture and lifestyle. In this chapter, we will delve into the vibrant traditions, festivals, and customs that shape the Portuguese way of life. From learning the language to discovering local cuisine, we will guide you on how to fully embrace the rich cultural heritage that surrounds you.

5.2 Navigating Everyday Life:

Adjusting to a new routine and daily life in a foreign country can be both exciting and challenging. This section will provide you with practical advice on navigating everyday tasks such as grocery shopping, transportation, healthcare services, and education. We will share tips and resources to help you smoothly transition into your new environment and make the most of your time in Portugal.

5.3 Building Your Network and Social Circle:

Creating a strong support system and building meaningful connections is essential for a successful and fulfilling life abroad. We will explore various avenues for expanding your social network, whether it's through joining local clubs, organisations, or expat communities. Discovering like-minded individuals and forming friendships will not only enhance your experience but also provide a sense of belonging and support as you embark on this new chapter.

5.4 Exploring the Wonders of Portugal:

Beyond the practicalities of everyday life, Portugal offers a wealth of captivating experiences and breathtaking destinations waiting to be explored. In this chapter, we will take you on a journey through the country's diverse landscapes, historic sites, and hidden gems. From the vibrant streets of Lisbon to the charming villages of the countryside, we will provide you with insider tips and recommendations to make the most of your adventures and create lasting memories in your new home.

As you embark on this exciting phase of your journey, remember that embracing change and maintaining an open mind are key to fully experiencing the wonders that Portugal has to offer. This section will serve as your guide and companion as you settle into your new life, ensuring that you make the most of your time in this enchanting corner of the world.

Chapter 6: "How To"

This chapter will give you checklists, "how to" information from getting a NIF to opening a bank account and applying for NHR and more. Plus some practical tips to help you navigate this wonderful journey and be a guide for when you feel daunted or overwhelmed.

Chapter 7: Moving to Portugal with Pets

Moving with your furry friends is possible with a little planning and understanding of the requirements so you can keep your family together and safe. It's possible to travel with your pets without quarantine as long as you meet all the requirements.

Chapter 8: The Portuguese Property Market: Opportunities and Challenges

The Portuguese property market has experienced significant growth in recent years, attracting both domestic and international buyers. However, it's essential to navigate this market with caution and be aware of potential pitfalls and challenges. In this chapter, we will explore the state of the Portuguese property market, discussing its opportunities, overpricing concerns, excess properties, and provide references to articles, research, and statistics to support our analysis.

Chapter 9: Exploring the Realities: Addressing the Downsides

While Portugal offers numerous advantages and a high quality of life, it's important to acknowledge and address some of the downsides or potential challenges you may encounter when moving to the country. It is essential to approach your new life in Portugal with realistic expectations and an understanding of the local dynamics.

Chapter 10: Useful websites, resources and more

A collated list of useful websites, resources, and YouTube channels to help you navigate life in Portugal.

So, let's dive in and uncover the endless possibilities that await you as you embark on your new life in Portugal!

1 UNVEILING THE MAGIC

1.1 Why Portugal?

Portugal, with its irresistible charm, has emerged as a sought-after destination for individuals seeking a fresh start and a place to call home. It's beauty, safety, high quality of life and it's favourable tax regime make it an enticing destination for anyone looking for a balanced and fulfilling lifestyle. This section aims to unveil the magic that captivates the imagination and draws people from all corners of the globe to the shores of Portugal.

A Tapestry of Natural Beauty

Portugal's natural landscapes are a tapestry of breathtaking beauty that enchants visitors and residents alike. From the sun-kissed golden beaches along the Algarve coast to the rugged cliffs of the Costa Vicentina, Portugal boasts a diverse coastline that stretches for over 1,800 kilometers. Whether you seek relaxation on pristine shores or crave exhilarating water sports, Portugal's beaches offer something for everyone.

Beyond the coastline, the country's interior is adorned with rolling hills, vineyards, and picturesque countryside. The Douro Valley, a UNESCO World Heritage site, showcases terraced vineyards and the winding Douro River, producing renowned wines that delight connoisseurs worldwide. The stunning landscapes of the Alentejo region invite you to explore their vast plains, cork forests, and charming traditional villages. From the volcanic wonders of the Azores to the rugged mountains of the Peneda-Gerês National Park, Portugal's natural beauty never fails to leave a lasting impression.

A Rich Tapestry of History and Culture

Portugal's history is a captivating tale woven through centuries, leaving a profound cultural legacy. As one of Europe's oldest nations, Portugal has a remarkable heritage showcased in its architecture, traditions, and way of life. The captivating cities of Lisbon, Porto, and Coimbra bear witness to the country's illustrious past, with their historical neighbourhoods, grand palaces, and majestic cathedrals.

The influence of the Portuguese explorers who set sail during the Age of Discovery is palpable throughout the country. The Maritime Museum in Lisbon and the Belém Tower stand as testaments to Portugal's seafaring prowess, while the University of Coimbra, founded in 1290, represents a rich academic history.

Traditional Portuguese music, such as fado, echoes through the narrow streets, expressing the soul of the nation. Festivals and cultural celebrations, like the Festa de São João in Porto or the Festa dos Tabuleiros in Tomar, offer a glimpse into the vibrant local traditions and a chance to immerse yourself in the joyous spirit of Portugal.

Gastronomic Delights and Culinary Traditions

Portugal is a haven for food lovers, renowned for its delectable cuisine and gastronomic traditions. From the mouthwatering flavours of bacalhau (salted codfish) to the fragrant pastéis de nata (custard tarts), Portuguese cuisine combines fresh ingredients, traditional recipes, and a touch of Mediterranean influence.

Each region of Portugal boasts its own culinary specialties, from the seafood treasures of the coastal regions to the hearty stews of the interior. Exploring the local markets, savouring regional wines, and indulging in traditional dishes is an essential part of the Portuguese experience.

Warmth, Hospitality, and a Relaxed Lifestyle

One of Portugal's greatest assets is its people, known for their warmth, hospitality, and relaxed approach to life. The Portuguese value family, friendship, and social connections, creating a strong sense of community and making it easier to integrate into the local way of life. Whether you're strolling through the colourful streets of Lisbon or enjoying a coffee in a cozy café, you'll often find the Portuguese taking the time to savour life's simple pleasures.

The country's laid-back lifestyle, combined with a favourable climate and abundant sunshine, promotes a slower pace and a focus on well-being. It's no wonder Portugal is often cited as one of the best places in the world to retire, offering a higher quality of life and a chance to savour every moment.

Portugal's allure lies in its captivating natural landscapes, rich history and culture, mouthwatering cuisine, and the warmth and hospitality of its people. It's a country that welcomes those seeking a fresh start and invites them to embrace a new chapter filled with beauty, tradition, and a relaxed way of life. Portugal truly holds the promise of an enchanting and fulfilling experience for those who choose to call it home.

Bucket List: Top 20 Things to Do, See, and Eat in Portugal

- Explore the vibrant neighbourhoods of Lisbon, including Alfama, Bairro Alto, and Belém.
- Wander through the fairytale-like streets of Sintra and visit the enchanting Pena Palace.
- Discover the historical charm of Porto while strolling along the Ribeira district and tasting the famous Port wine.
- Relax on the stunning beaches of the Algarve, such as Praia da Marinha or Praia do Camilo.
- Experience the magical atmosphere of Fado, Portugal's soulful traditional music, in a Lisbon tavern.
- Marvel at the mystical beauty of the Azores archipelago, with its volcanic landscapes and breathtaking hiking trails.
- Visit the iconic Tower of Belém and the Jerónimos Monastery, UNESCO World Heritage sites in Lisbon.
- Indulge in the delicious pastéis de nata, Portugal's famous custard tarts, preferably from the original Pastéis de Belém bakery.
- Take a boat trip along the Douro River and admire the terraced vineyards that produce the renowned Port wine.
- Explore the picturesque villages of the Alentejo region, such as Monsaraz and Évora, and immerse yourself in their rich

history.

- Experience the lively atmosphere of traditional markets, such as Mercado da Ribeira in Lisbon or Mercado Bolhão in Porto.
- Visit the historic university town of Coimbra and explore its magnificent library, Biblioteca Joanina.
- Embark on a scenic road trip along the stunning coastline of the Costa Vicentina, stopping at hidden beaches and charming fishing villages.
- Hike through the natural beauty of Peneda-Gerês National Park and discover its waterfalls, lakes, and wildlife.
- Dive into the local gastronomy by indulging in fresh seafood dishes like grilled sardines or a hearty cataplana stew.
- Witness the grandeur of the Roman ruins in Conímbriga and the historical city walls of Évora.
- Experience the colourful liveliness of traditional festivals, such as the Festival of São João in Porto or the Carnaval in Torres Vedras.
- Visit the charming village of Óbidos, surrounded by medieval walls, and enjoy a sip of Ginja, a traditional cherry liqueur.
- Discover the natural wonders of the Berlengas Islands, an archipelago off the coast of Peniche, known for its pristine beaches and diverse marine life.
- Take a scenic train ride along the Douro Valley, admiring the vineyards and landscapes, and perhaps enjoy a wine tasting along the way.

This bucket list encompasses a diverse range of experiences that showcase the natural beauty, cultural heritage, and culinary delights that Portugal has to offer. From exploring historical landmarks to savouring traditional dishes and immersing yourself in the vibrant local traditions, these experiences will leave you with unforgettable memories of your time in Portugal.

A fun fact about Lisbon is that it is home to an impressive number of museums. In fact, the city boasts over 50 museums, offering a diverse range of cultural, historical, and artistic experiences for visitors and locals alike. From the renowned National Museum of Ancient Art, which houses an extensive collection of Portuguese art, to the interactive and engaging Lisbon Story Centre, which takes visitors on a journey through the city's history, there is something for everyone to explore and enjoy.

Whether you have a passion for art, archaeology, science, or even maritime history, Lisbon's museum scene offers a fascinating glimpse into the rich heritage and vibrant culture of the city.

1.2 The Joys of the Portuguese Lifestyle

From the moment you arrive, you'll be enveloped in the warm hospitality of the Portuguese people, who are known for their friendly and welcoming nature. Whether it's striking up a conversation with a local in a café or being invited to join in a lively conversation during a traditional festival, you'll experience firsthand the genuine warmth and openness of the Portuguese.

As you settle into your new home, you'll discover the joy of embracing a slower, more relaxed pace of life. The Portuguese have mastered the art of enjoying the present moment, savouring each experience with a laid-back and unhurried approach. One of the most delightful aspects of the Portuguese lifestyle is the tradition of the siesta, a cherished time in the afternoon when the hustle and bustle of everyday life temporarily slows down. Embracing this cultural norm allows you to unwind, recharge, and fully appreciate the simple pleasures of life.

Indulging in the Portuguese culinary scene is an integral part of experiencing the local lifestyle. From the aroma of freshly baked bread in the morning to the delectable seafood feasts in seaside towns, the country's cuisine is a delightful reflection of its rich cultural heritage. The Portuguese take pride in their gastronomic traditions, and you'll find a vast array of mouthwatering dishes to tantalise your taste buds. From tasting traditional bacalhau (salted cod), sampling the diverse flavours of regional cheeses, or treating yourself to a glass of Vinho Verde on a sunny terrace, every meal is an opportunity to immerse yourself in the richness of Portuguese flavours.

Beyond the culinary delights, the Portuguese lifestyle is infused with a love for art, music, and celebration. From the soulful melodies of Fado, which tell tales of love, longing, and saudade, to the vibrant street festivals that bring communities together, you'll witness the profound connection the Portuguese have to their cultural heritage. Art and history are celebrated in every corner of the country, with museums, galleries, and beautifully preserved architectural marvels that offer glimpses into Portugal's fascinating past.

The joys of the Portuguese lifestyle lie in its people, traditions, and the simple pleasures that are cherished and celebrated daily. So, embrace the warm hospitality, slow down and enjoy the siesta-filled afternoons, and let the flavours, sounds, and vibrant culture of Portugal envelop you in a truly unforgettable experience.

Gentle words of wisdom

While the laid-back way of life in Portugal has its undeniable charm, it can present a few challenges for those coming from more fast-paced and structured environments, such as the UK or the USA. One potential downside is the concept of "Portuguese time," where schedules and deadlines may not be as rigidly adhered to as one might be accustomed to. This can sometimes lead to delays and there's a more relaxed attitude towards punctuality. As an expatriate, it's important to be aware of this cultural difference and adjust your expectations accordingly.

To navigate these cultural differences and ensure a smooth transition, it can be helpful to adopt a flexible mindset and practice patience. Embrace the slower pace of life and use the extra time to appreciate the surroundings or engage in meaningful conversations with locals. However, if you do have time-sensitive commitments, it's advisable to communicate your expectations clearly and proactively to avoid any misunderstandings.

To further aid in understanding and adjusting to the Portuguese way of life, there are resources available that provide valuable insights and tips. The book "Culture Smart! Portugal" by Sandy Guedes de Queiroz offers cultural guidance, etiquette tips, and practical advice for interacting effectively in Portuguese society. Additionally, websites and forums such as Expats Portugal and Internations provide platforms for expatriates to connect, share experiences, and seek advice from fellow expats who have navigated the cultural nuances of living in Portugal.

Remember, embracing a new culture means embracing both the

upsides and downsides. By acknowledging and respecting the differences in the laid-back Portuguese lifestyle, you can adapt and integrate more smoothly into your new surroundings, forging meaningful connections and enjoying the richness of the local culture. As Portuguese writer José Saramago once said, "You have to take risks. We will only understand the miracle of life fully when we allow the unexpected to happen."

1.3 The Great Escape: Seeking an Elevated Quality of Life

Discover why Portugal consistently ranks highly in global quality of life indexes, offering an enticing escape for those seeking an enhanced standard of living. With a focus on exceptional healthcare, safety, and overall well-being, Portugal offers a host of benefits that await those making it their new home.

Portugal's healthcare system is renowned for its quality and accessibility. According to the World Health Organisation (WHO), Portugal's healthcare system ranks 12th in the world, surpassing many other developed nations. The country boasts a robust network of hospitals, clinics, and healthcare professionals that provide comprehensive and affordable care to residents and expatriates alike. The Portuguese government's commitment to ensuring universal healthcare coverage contributes to a high level of health security for its population.

In addition to its exceptional public healthcare system, Portugal also offers a well-developed private medical sector that provides an alternative for those seeking specialised care or a higher level of service. Private healthcare providers offer a wide range of services, including specialised consultations, diagnostic tests, and elective procedures. Many expatriates and affluent residents choose private healthcare options for their efficiency, personalised attention, and shorter waiting times. While private healthcare in Portugal can come at a higher cost, it provides an additional layer of choice and convenience. (Please note that depending on your route to Portugal, your VISA requirements may stipulate that you must have private medical cover on arrival.)

Whilst this is not to be read as a ranking, here are some of the well-known private medical insurance carriers in Portugal:

1. Médis is a prominent private health insurance provider in Portugal, offering a range of comprehensive health plans. They provide coverage for medical consultations, diagnostic tests, hospitalisation, and other healthcare services. Médis is known for its extensive network of healthcare providers and personalised customer support.

2. Multicare is another major player in the private health insurance market in Portugal. They offer a variety of health insurance plans tailored to individuals, families, and companies. Multicare focuses on providing a wide range of coverage options, including outpatient care, hospitalisation, dental services, and preventive healthcare.

3. AdvanceCare is a leading private health insurance company that partners with various healthcare providers across Portugal. They offer health plans designed to meet the specific needs of individuals and companies. AdvanceCare provides coverage for medical consultations, exams, surgeries, and other medical treatments.

4. Allianz Care is a global health insurance provider with a presence in Portugal. They offer international health insurance plans that provide coverage not only in Portugal but also worldwide. Allianz Care offers flexible coverage options, including outpatient care, hospitalisation, emergency services, and specialist consultations.

5. Tranquilidade is a well-established insurance company in Portugal that provides a range of insurance products, including private health insurance. They offer health plans with different levels of coverage, allowing individuals and families to select the most suitable option for their needs. Tranquilidade focuses on delivering reliable coverage and personalised customer service.

Please note that this list is not exhaustive, and the availability and rankings of private medical insurance carriers may vary over time. It's recommended to research and compare different providers to find the one that best suits your specific requirements and preferences.

The top 5 private medical providers* in Portugal, known for their quality healthcare services and extensive network of facilities, include the following:

CUF is one of the largest private healthcare providers in Portugal, offering a comprehensive range of medical services across various specialties. With multiple hospitals and clinics located throughout the country, CUF is known for its state-of-the-art technology, highly skilled medical professionals, and patient-centred approach.

Luz Saúde is another prominent private healthcare group in Portugal. It operates a network of hospitals, clinics, and diagnostic centres, providing a wide range of medical services. Luz Saúde focuses on delivering personalised care, advanced medical treatments, and cutting-edge technologies to ensure optimal patient outcomes.

José de Mello Saúde is a leading healthcare provider in Portugal with a strong presence in both public and private sectors. It operates several renowned private hospitals and clinics, offering a broad spectrum of medical specialties and services. The group is recognised for its commitment to medical excellence, innovation, and patient satisfaction.

Lusíadas Saúde is a well-established private healthcare network that operates hospitals, clinics, and laboratories across Portugal. With a focus on patient-centred care, Lusíadas Saúde provides a comprehensive range of medical services, including specialised consultations, surgeries, and diagnostic tests.

Hospital da Luz is a prestigious private hospital renowned for its high-quality healthcare services. It combines modern facilities, cutting-edge technology, and a multidisciplinary team of healthcare professionals to deliver advanced medical treatments and personalised care. Hospital da Luz is recognised for its expertise in various medical specialties, including cardiology, oncology, and orthopaedics.

These private medical providers are known for their

commitment to medical excellence, patient satisfaction, and the ability to deliver comprehensive and specialised healthcare services to residents and expatriates in Portugal. It's important to note that the availability of specific providers may vary depending on the region within Portugal.

This list is correct to the best of my knowledge at the time of writing.

When it comes to safety, Portugal also shines. The Global Peace Index consistently ranks Portugal among the top 5 safest countries in the world. With low crime rates, efficient law enforcement, and a peaceful social environment, residents can enjoy a sense of security and peace of mind in their daily lives. Whether exploring the vibrant city streets or strolling through the tranquil countryside, Portugal's commitment to safety creates a welcoming and secure environment for all.

Furthermore, Portugal's overall well-being is reflected in its emphasis on work-life balance and the pursuit of happiness. In the United Nations' World Happiness Report, Portugal consistently ranks among the top countries in terms of happiness and life satisfaction. The Portuguese embrace a slower pace of life, allowing time for leisure, family, and personal fulfilment. The country's natural beauty, including its stunning coastlines, charming towns, and picturesque landscapes, provides ample opportunities for outdoor activities, relaxation, and a deep connection with nature.

By choosing Portugal as your new home, you are embarking on a journey toward an elevated quality of life. From the exceptional healthcare system and strong emphasis on safety to the overall well-being and happiness of its residents, Portugal offers a supportive and enriching environment. As you delve deeper into the Portuguese way of life, you will come to appreciate the numerous benefits that contribute to a truly fulfilling experience in your new home.

2 PREPARING FOR THE JOURNEY

2.1 Assessing Your Motivations: Defining Your Purpose

Before you set off on the path to Portugal, it's important to take a moment to assess your motivations and define your purpose for making this life-altering decision. Understanding your underlying goals and aspirations will serve as a compass, guiding you through the process and helping you make informed choices along the way. And helping you to stay the course when things get challenging.

One key motivation for many individuals considering a move to Portugal is the allure of a change of scenery. Whether you seek a new adventure, a different climate, or an escape from the familiar, Portugal certainly offers you all the above. Is that enough for you to leave behind the familiar?

Another aspect to consider is the potential for career opportunities. Portugal has been experiencing a growing economy and an increasing number of international companies setting up operations within its borders. Whether you are looking to launch a new business venture, pursue a job in a specific field, or take advantage of remote work opportunities, Portugal's thriving business environment and entrepreneurial spirit can be a catalyst for professional growth.

For many, the desire for a slower pace of life is a significant motivation for relocating to Portugal. The Portuguese embrace a relaxed and laid-back lifestyle, where taking time to savour life's simple pleasures and cultivating meaningful relationships are highly valued. If you yearn for a more balanced and fulfilling existence, Portugal's cultural ethos and emphasis on work-life balance can provide the ideal setting for your aspirations.

As you embark on your journey to Portugal, take the time to delve into your motivations, exploring what drives you and what you hope to achieve in your new life. Reflect on your personal and professional goals, the type of lifestyle you envision, and the experiences you seek. This introspection will not only shape your decision-making process but also help you align your actions with your true purpose, ensuring a more fulfilling and rewarding transition to your new life in Portugal. Remember, as American author Mark Twain once said, "The secret of success is making your vocation your vacation."

2.2 Researching and Selecting Your Destination

Portugal's appeal lies not only in its countrywide charm but also in its diverse regions, each offering a unique lifestyle and atmosphere. As you embark on the journey of moving to Portugal, it is crucial to research and select a destination that aligns with your preferences and aspirations, creating the perfect backdrop for your new life.

Lisbon, the capital city, stands as a vibrant and cosmopolitan hub that blends history with modernity. Its bustling streets, charming neighbourhoods, and lively cultural scene make it a sought-after destination for those craving the energy of urban living. Lisbon's international appeal is evident in the growing expat community that calls this city home. According to a report by Portugal Resident, Lisbon boasts a high concentration of expats, particularly in neighbourhoods such as Chiado, Principe Real, and Alfama. The city's infrastructure, transport links, and abundance of amenities make it an ideal choice for professionals, creatives, and those seeking a bustling city life.

For those in search of tranquil coastal living, the Algarve region presents an enticing option. With its picturesque beaches, breathtaking cliffs, and laid-back lifestyle, the Algarve has become a haven for expats looking to enjoy the sun, sea, and a slower pace of life. According to a survey conducted by The Portugal News, the Algarve region is home to a significant expat community, particularly in areas such as Faro, Albufeira, and Lagos. Expats are drawn to the region's warm climate, outdoor activities, and a welcoming community that embraces both locals and internationals.

Porto, the second-largest city in Portugal, offers a captivating blend of history, culture, and charm. Known for its iconic bridges, narrow streets, and world-famous port wine, Porto is a cultural treasure trove. It has also been gaining attention as an emerging destination for expats. The Portugal News highlights the growth of the expat community in Porto, attracted by its architectural beauty, thriving arts scene, and affordable cost of living compared to other European cities.

When selecting your destination in Portugal, it is vital to consider factors such as climate, cost of living, proximity to amenities, cultural offerings, and access to transportation. When it comes to the weather, the Algarve is a popular tourist destination as it has higher temperatures (it makes for a busy high season). The west coast and middle of the country has comfortable summer temperatures, breezy days, more rain and it's milder by the ocean. The north and the interior have much chillier winters, there's even a dusting of snow in the Serra Da Estrela Mountains.

Do your research and local resources like expat forums, online communities, Facbook Groups, YouTube channels and city guides can provide valuable insights and firsthand experiences from those who have already made the move. Additionally, consulting official government websites, such as the Portuguese Immigration and Borders Service (SEF), can provide up-to-date information on residency requirements and regulations.

By conducting thorough research and taking into account your preferences and aspirations, you can identify the region in Portugal that best suits your desired lifestyle. Whether you choose the vibrant cityscape of Lisbon, the serene coastal towns of the

Algarve, or the cultural heritage of Porto, each region has its own distinctive character that promises a fulfilling and enriching experience as you embark on your new journey in Portugal.

2.3 Financial Considerations and Budgeting

Embarking on a journey to Portugal requires careful financial planning and budgeting to ensure a seamless transition to your new life. Understanding the cost of living, taxation system, healthcare expenses, and other financial considerations will help you make informed decisions and maintain financial stability during your move.

Cost of Living: Portugal is known for offering a relatively affordable cost of living compared to many other European countries. However, it is essential to consider the specific region you plan to reside in, as costs can vary. Cities like Lisbon and Porto generally have higher living expenses compared to smaller towns and rural areas. It's advisable to research and compare factors such as housing prices, transportation costs, groceries, utilities, and leisure activities to estimate your budget accurately.

Taxation: Portugal has a progressive tax system that considers different income brackets. In recent years, Portugal has also introduced various tax incentives to attract foreign residents, such as the Non-Habitual Resident (NHR) program.

Non-Habitual Resident (NHR) Tax Regime: The NHR tax regime is a popular choice for many UK and USA citizens moving to Portugal. It offers significant tax benefits for qualifying individuals, including a flat tax rate of 20% on certain types of foreign-sourced income, such as pensions, dividends, and royalties. This regime can be particularly advantageous for retirees and individuals with significant foreign income. To qualify for the NHR status, you must meet specific requirements and adhere to the guidelines set by the Portuguese tax authorities. Seeking professional advice from a tax consultant or lawyer specialising in international taxation is recommended to ensure compliance and maximise the benefits of this program.

Healthcare Expenses: Portugal boasts a high-quality healthcare system, offering both public and private options. As a resident, you will have access to the public healthcare system through the National Health Service (SNS). The SNS provides affordable or even free healthcare services, including consultations, hospitalisations, and prescription medications. Private health insurance is also available for additional coverage and faster access to medical services. It is important to consider the costs of private health insurance premiums, deductibles, and co-payments when budgeting for healthcare expenses.

Other Financial Considerations: When moving to Portugal, it is crucial to account for additional financial factors. These may include visa and residency permit fees, relocation costs, transportation expenses, banking charges, insurance premiums, and any potential currency exchange fees. Building an emergency fund to cover unexpected expenses or unforeseen circumstances is also advisable.

Resources: To gain a comprehensive understanding of the financial considerations when moving to Portugal, it is recommended to consult reliable sources and seek professional advice. The Portuguese Tax and Customs Authority (Autoridade Tributária e Aduaneira) provides information on tax regulations and residency-related matters. The Portuguese government's official website (www.portugal.gov.pt) offers valuable resources and links to government services. Expatriate forums and online communities, such as expat groups on social media platforms, can also provide insights and personal experiences from individuals who have already made the move.

By carefully considering the financial aspects, creating a realistic budget, and seeking expert advice, you can effectively plan for your financial well-being and ensure a smooth transition to your new life in Portugal. Understanding the costs involved and making informed decisions will contribute to a more secure and enjoyable experience as you embrace all that Portugal has to offer.

Word of Caution: Seeking Reliable Advice

When navigating the financial considerations of moving to Portugal, it is essential to exercise caution and discernment when seeking advice. While expert guidance can be invaluable, it is important to be mindful of potential scams, overcharging, or misinformation from unscrupulous individuals posing as professionals.

One common area where caution is warranted is when dealing with solicitors or consultants who may overcharge for simple tasks that can be researched and addressed independently. While there are reputable professionals who can provide valuable assistance, it is advisable to conduct thorough research, compare prices, and seek recommendations from reliable sources before engaging their services.

To avoid falling victim to misleading information or excessive fees, consider the following tips:

1. Research and Educate Yourself: Take the time to gather information from reliable sources, such as official government websites, reputable publications, and recognised financial institutions. Familiarise yourself with the basics of the processes and requirements involved in moving to Portugal. This knowledge will empower you to make informed decisions and identify when advice aligns with the established guidelines. The information is available.

2. Seek Recommendations: Consult with trusted individuals who have successfully gone through a similar process of moving to Portugal. They can provide insights into their own experiences, recommend trustworthy professionals they worked with, and offer valuable tips to help you avoid potential pitfalls.

3. Obtain Multiple Quotes: When engaging professional services, whether it's for legal advice, financial consultation, or other related matters, request quotes from multiple providers. This allows you to compare prices, services offered, and the reputation of each provider. Beware of significantly higher or unusually low fees, and consider seeking clarification on the breakdown of costs.

4. Check Credentials and Reviews: Before hiring any professional, thoroughly research their credentials, qualifications, and reputation. Look for certifications, memberships in

professional organisations, and positive reviews or testimonials from previous clients. Consider checking online platforms and forums where expats share their experiences to gather insights into the reputability of specific service providers.

5. Trust Your Instincts: If something feels off or you sense any pressure tactics, be cautious. Trusted professionals will provide clear and transparent information, answer your questions patiently, and respect your decision-making process. If you encounter any red flags, consider seeking advice from an alternative source or consulting with multiple professionals to gain a well-rounded perspective.

While it is advisable to seek expert advice, it is equally important to exercise due diligence and be cautious when entrusting your financial matters to others. By researching, obtaining multiple quotes, checking credentials, and trusting your instincts, you can better protect yourself against potential scams, charlatans, or unnecessary expenses. Remember, knowledge and prudence are key in navigating the financial aspects of your move to Portugal.

3 NAVIGATING THE LEGAL LANDSCAPE

3.1 Visa and Residency Options

Understanding the visa and residency requirements is crucial when considering a move to Portugal from the UK or USA. This section will provide an overview of the various visa options available, ensuring you have a clear understanding of the pathways to legal residency in Portugal.

As a non-EU member, there are several main visa entry types available to enter Portugal. Here's a brief overview of these visa types:

Schengen Visa: The Schengen Visa allows for short-term stays in Portugal and other Schengen Area countries for tourism, business, or family visits. This visa is typically valid for a maximum of 90 days within a 180-day period.

D-Type Visa: The D-Type Visa is a long-stay visa that allows individuals to reside in Portugal for a specific purpose, such as work, study, family reunification, or research (D2, D3. D4, D6, D7 and D9). This visa is generally issued for stays longer than 90 days and requires additional documentation and supporting evidence based on the purpose of the stay.

The D2 visa is designed for those seeking self-employment or entrepreneurship opportunities in the country. The D3 visa is suitable for students pursuing higher education in Portugal. The D4 visa caters to individuals who wish to work in Portugal, while the D7 visa is ideal for those with passive income sources. The D6 visa, known as the Family Reunification Visa, allows family members of Portuguese citizens or foreign residents to join their loved ones in Portugal. The D9 Retirement Visa, for retirees looking to relocate to Portugal. Each visa has its specific requirements and benefits, catering to different motivations and circumstances of individuals seeking to live and work in Portugal.

Golden Visa Program*: The Golden Visa program is a residence-by-investment program. It is designed for non-EU citizens who make a qualifying investment in the country, such as purchasing real estate, creating jobs, or making a capital transfer. The program offers a fast-track route to residency and eventual citizenship. The specific investment requirements and eligibility criteria vary, so it is crucial to consult official government sources and seek legal advice to understand the latest regulations and any recent changes to the program.

*At the time of writing this, it has been reported that the Golden Visa program is set to expire at some point by the end of 2023.

Work Visa: The Work Visa is designed for individuals who have secured employment in Portugal. It requires a job offer from a Portuguese employer and often involves a sponsorship process by the employer. The Work Visa allows for legal residence and work authorisation in the country.

Digital Nomad Visa: Portugal has recently introduced a new visa option specifically tailored for digital nomads. The Digital Nomad Visa allows remote workers to legally reside in Portugal while maintaining their employment with companies outside the country. This visa is designed for individuals who have the flexibility to work remotely and wish to experience the Portuguese lifestyle and culture. The requirements for the Digital Nomad Visa typically include proof of remote employment, sufficient financial means to support oneself, and health insurance coverage. It offers a unique opportunity for individuals to combine work and leisure in a vibrant and welcoming country. The Digital Nomad Visa reflects

Portugal's commitment to attracting professionals from around the world who contribute to the local economy while enjoying the benefits of living in Portugal. It is advisable to consult the official Portuguese immigration website or contact the Portuguese Embassy or Consulate for the most up-to-date information and specific requirements related to the Digital Nomad Visa.

Residence Permit Application Process: Apart from the NHR and Golden Visa programs, UK and USA citizens can explore other residency permit options, such as obtaining a residence permit based on employment, entrepreneurship, family reunification, or study. Each category has its own specific requirements, and the application process may involve submitting documentation, undergoing background checks, and attending interviews. It is advisable to consult the Portuguese Immigration and Borders Service (SEF) website to understand the eligibility criteria and procedural steps involved in each residency permit category. You can also contact the Consulate in your home country and obtain the most accurate and up-to-date information regarding the visa entry types and their specific eligibility criteria.

Further Resources:

- Portuguese Immigration and Borders Service (SEF): The SEF website (www.sef.pt) provides official information on immigration and residency matters in Portugal. It offers guidance, forms, and updates on visa requirements, residence permits, and relevant legislation.

- Embassy or Consulate: Contact the Portuguese Embassy or Consulate in your home country for accurate and up-to-date information regarding visa and residency options. They can provide guidance, answer specific queries, and assist with the application process.

- Legal Professionals: Engaging the services of an immigration lawyer or specialist who is knowledgeable about Portuguese immigration laws and experienced in assisting UK and USA citizens can be beneficial. They can provide personalised advice, help navigate the legal landscape, and ensure compliance with all requirements.

Please note that I personally don't recommend necessarily seeking the help of a legal professional (your personal situation and complexity aside). It was my personal experience that the lawyers we used didn't do a lot, in fact if it wasn't for my own research I would have failed on my application as they had omitted key instructions and documents. My best advice is to educate your self, talk to people who have done it before you. It really isn't rocket science. I have heard first hand accounts of individuals who paid north of €20,000 for a lawyer to guide them through the D7 visa application when all the time their spouse was an Irish passport holder and therefore EU citizen. Please proceed with caution when seeking advice.

Understanding the visa and residency options available is crucial to making an informed decision about your relocation to Portugal. By familiarising yourself with the Non-Habitual Resident (NHR) tax regime, the Golden Visa program, and other residency permit categories, you can better navigate the legal requirements and ensure a smooth transition to your new life in Portugal.

D7 Pathway to residency and citizenship

The D-Type Visa requires applicants to provide detailed documentation and meet specific requirements based on the purpose of their stay. For example, individuals applying for a work visa must have a job offer from a Portuguese employer and meet certain qualifications. Students seeking to pursue higher education in Portugal need to provide acceptance letters from recognised educational institutions. Family reunification visas require proof of relationship with a Portuguese resident or citizen. And the 'passive income' visa requires you to show proof of earnings from financial investments, dividends, pension or rental income.

The application process involves submitting the necessary forms, supporting documents, and payment of applicable fees. The D-Type Visa grants individuals the right to reside in Portugal for a longer duration, typically exceeding 90 days, and may be subject to renewal or conversion into a residence permit once in the country. As a popular choice, let's go through the D7 Visa checklist.

Checklist for the D7 Passive Income Visa for Portugal:

1. Proof of Income: Gather all necessary documentation to demonstrate a consistent and regular source of passive income. This can include bank statements, investment portfolios, rental income statements, pension statements, or any other relevant financial documents.

2. Minimum Income Requirement: Ensure that your passive income meets the minimum income requirement set by the Portuguese government. As of the current regulations, the minimum income required is calculated at 12 times the Portuguese national minimum wage (as of the year 2021), subject to periodic adjustments. It is advisable to check the latest income requirements on the official Portuguese immigration website or consult with the Portuguese Embassy or Consulate in your home country.

3. Health Insurance: Obtain health insurance coverage that is valid in Portugal. The insurance should provide comprehensive medical coverage during your stay in Portugal and meet the requirements set by the Portuguese authorities. Ensure that the insurance policy covers hospitalisation, emergencies, and any other necessary medical expenses.

4. Criminal Record Certificate: Obtain a criminal record certificate from your home country or countries where you have resided in the past few years. This certificate should be issued by the relevant authorities and indicate that you have no criminal convictions. The document may need to be translated into Portuguese and possibly apostilled or legalised, depending on the requirements.

5. Proof of Accommodation: Provide evidence of suitable accommodation in Portugal. This can include a lease agreement, property ownership documents, or a letter from a host stating their willingness to accommodate you during your stay. The accommodation should comply with the requirements set by the Portuguese authorities.

6. Application Forms: Complete the required application forms for the D7 Passive Income Visa. These forms can be obtained from the Portuguese Embassy or Consulate or downloaded from the

official Portuguese immigration website. Fill out the forms accurately and ensure that all required fields are completed.

7. Passport and Photos: Ensure that your passport is valid for the duration of your intended stay in Portugal. Make copies of your passport and provide recent passport-sized photos as per the specifications provided by the Portuguese authorities.

8. Application Fee: Pay the applicable visa application fee. The fee may vary depending on your nationality and the current regulations. Check the official Portuguese immigration website or contact the Portuguese Embassy or Consulate for the updated fee information.

9. Additional Documents: Review the specific requirements for the D7 Passive Income Visa and gather any additional documents that may be requested. These could include proof of education, proof of ties to Portugal (if applicable), or any other supporting documents relevant to your case.

10. Submitting the Application: Once you have gathered all the necessary documents, submit your completed application, along with the supporting documents and payment of the application fee, to the Portuguese Embassy or Consulate in your home country. Follow their guidelines regarding submission methods, appointment requirements, and processing times.

It is important to note that visa requirements and procedures may change over time, so it is recommended to consult the SEF website (https://imigrante.sef.pt/en/)

4 MAKING THE MOVE

4.1 Packing and Logistics: What to Bring and What to Leave Behind

When it comes to making the move to Portugal, deciding what to bring and what to leave behind can be a daunting process. In this section, we'll provide you with practical tips to help minimise the stress and make your packing and logistics smoother. Firstly, it's essential to consider the climate and lifestyle in Portugal. Pack appropriate clothing for the different seasons and outdoor activities you plan to enjoy. Remember to also research the voltage and plug types in Portugal, as you might need to bring adapters for your electronic devices.

When it comes to shipping your belongings, it's advisable to compare quotes from different international moving companies and consider their reputation, reliability, and customer reviews. Take inventory of your items and consider whether it's more cost-effective to ship them or purchase new ones in Portugal. If you're leaving behind furniture or other large items, you may explore options for selling, donating, or storing them.

Understanding customs regulations is crucial to avoid any complications when bringing your belongings into Portugal. Research the prohibited and restricted items, such as certain electronics, firearms, or certain food products, to ensure compliance. Familiarise yourself with the customs declaration process and any required paperwork or documentation.

Additionally, it's worth considering the option of temporary accommodation upon your arrival in Portugal. Renting a furnished apartment or staying in a short-term rental can provide you with time to settle in, explore different neighbourhoods, and make an informed decision about your long-term housing needs.

To make your packing and logistics smoother, here are some useful resources to consult:

1. The official website of the Portuguese Customs Authority (Autoridade Tributária e Aduaneira): This website provides information on customs regulations, prohibited items, and any required documentation.

2. International moving companies: Research reputable international moving companies and obtain quotes from multiple providers to compare services and prices.

3. Online expat forums and communities: Join online communities and forums where you can connect with expats who have already made the move to Portugal. They can provide valuable advice and insights based on their own experiences.

4. Storage facilities: If you need to store some of your belongings before or after your move, research local storage facilities in Portugal that offer secure and convenient options.

By following these tips and utilising the available resources, you can navigate the packing and logistics process with greater ease and ensure a smoother transition to your new life in Portugal.

4.2 Finding Accommodation: Renting, Buying, and Temporary Stays

Securing suitable accommodation is a crucial aspect of your relocation to Portugal. In this section, we'll provide you with valuable insights into Portugal's rental and real estate markets, guiding you through the process of finding accommodation that suits your needs and preferences.

If you're considering renting a property in Portugal, it's essential to understand the rental market dynamics. Rental prices can vary depending on the location, property size, and amenities. Popular cities like Lisbon and Porto tend to have higher rental costs compared to smaller towns and rural areas. Researching different neighbourhoods and their characteristics can help you identify the best fit for your lifestyle and budget.

To begin your search for rental properties, online platforms such as idealista.pt, casa.sapo.pt, and olx.pt are popular resources. These platforms offer a wide range of rental listings across Portugal, allowing you to filter your search based on criteria such as location, price, and property type. Engaging with local real estate agencies or independent property owners can also provide you with additional options and insights. (I will include a longer list of real estate websites later in the book).

If you're considering buying a property in Portugal, it's advisable to work with a reputable real estate agent who specialises in the local market. They can help you navigate the buying process, including property search, negotiation, and legal procedures. Be mindful of additional costs such as property transfer tax, stamp duty, and legal fees, which should be factored into your budget.

As a side note when it comes to property, when you've decided on your area of choice call a few agents and ask them what the average price per square meter is in that region. This is going to help you to calculate what price you should be paying and help you to make an offer inline with the market value. I know that sounds obvious however it's not uncommon to see prices of properties varying as much as €100,000 from website to website. Property prices have been pushed up undoubtedly by demand from foreigners and the Golden Visa program and so on, therefore it's important to make sure you're not paying over market value and contributing to the problem.

For those who prefer temporary housing options upon arrival, Portugal offers a variety of choices. Apart-hotels, serviced apartments, and guesthouses provide the convenience of temporary stays with the flexibility to search for long-term accommodation once you're on the ground. Websites such as booking.com, Airbnb, and HomeAway offer a wide selection of temporary housing options, allowing you to choose based on location, duration, and amenities.

It's important to consider factors such as proximity to amenities, public transportation, healthcare facilities, and safety when selecting accommodation. Additionally, be sure to read and understand the terms of rental or purchase agreements, and ask any relevant questions before committing to a property.

Please be mindful that VISA requirements such as the D-Type visa require you to have accommodation as part of your application process. It's important to ensure the lease you're provided with complies with your application.

Here are some additional resources to assist you in finding accommodation in Portugal:

1. Real estate agencies: Research and engage with reputable real estate agencies that specialise in the region where you're looking to rent or buy property (there's a full list of realtor websites later in this guide).

2. Local classifieds and newspapers: Check local classifieds in newspapers or online platforms for property listings and contact details.

3. Expat forums and social media groups: Join expat forums and social media groups focused on Portugal, where you can connect with fellow expats and seek advice and recommendations on accommodation.

4. Local networking events: Attend local networking events or expat meet ups in Portugal to connect with people who have firsthand knowledge of the housing market. (I've known people to find their perfect property from chatting to people in coffee shops!)

By utilising these resources and being proactive in your search, you can find suitable accommodation that aligns with your preferences and ensures a smooth transition to your new life in Portugal.

4.3 Settling In: Establishing Networks and Connecting with the Community

Building a support network and connecting with the local community is an integral part of settling into your new life in Portugal. Here are some valuable tips to help you establish networks and immerse yourself in the vibrant Portuguese community:

1. Language Learning: While many Portuguese people speak English, learning the local language, Portuguese, can greatly enhance your integration and communication with the local community. Take advantage of language learning resources such as language courses, language exchange programs, online platforms, and mobile apps to improve your language skills.

Here's a little side note and tip from personal experience, if you use an app to learn Portuguese make sure it's European Portuguese! Brazilian is somewhat different in terms of vocabulary and pronunciation. I recommend Practice Portuguese - https://www.practiceportuguese.com/

Adding to this, there are free Portuguese courses available usually in your local library or school. You'll need your resident permit to apply. Search for the Portuguese Language Learning Promotion Office (GLPt).

2. Expatriate Associations: Joining expatriate associations or groups can be an excellent way to meet fellow expats who share similar experiences and challenges. These associations often organise social events, cultural activities, and networking opportunities, providing a supportive community for newcomers. Explore organisations such as the American Club of Lisbon or the British-Portuguese Chamber of Commerce.

3. Social Media and Online Communities: Connect with like-minded individuals and access valuable information. Join expat

groups or forums specific to your location or interests, where you can ask questions, seek advice, and participate in events and activities.

4. Local Clubs and Organisations: Get involved in local clubs, organisations, or hobby groups that align with your interests. Whether it's joining a sports team, participating in art classes, yoga on the beach or volunteering for a cause, these activities can help you meet locals and establish meaningful connections.

5. Cultural Events and Festivals: Portugal is known for its vibrant cultural scene, with numerous festivals, concerts, exhibitions, and celebrations throughout the year. Attend local events and immerse yourself in the rich Portuguese culture to gain a deeper understanding of the country and connect with the local community.

6. Community Workshops and Classes: Enrol in community workshops or classes that interest you, such as cooking, dancing, or crafts. These activities provide opportunities to interact with locals and learn about Portuguese traditions and customs. (I've used the opportunity to try new things and even found that I quite enjoyed a pottery class and met new people).

7. Networking Events: Keep an eye out for networking events, business conferences, and professional gatherings in your area. These events offer a platform to meet professionals from various industries, expand your professional network, and potentially discover career opportunities.

8. Volunteer Work: Engaging in volunteer work can be a fulfilling way to contribute to the local community and meet people who share your passion for making a positive impact. Research local charities, non-profit organisations, or community centres that welcome volunteers.

9. Expat Publications and Blogs: Stay informed about local events, cultural insights, and expat experiences by reading expat publications and blogs dedicated to life in Portugal. Listen to the radio, podcasts and TV or YouTube channels in Portuguese.

5 YOUR NEW LIFE IN PORTUGAL

Embracing the culture and lifestyle of Portugal is an enriching experience that allows you to fully immerse yourself in the vibrant traditions and customs of your new home. Here are some tips, resources, and suggestions to help you make the most of your cultural exploration:

1. Discover Local Cuisine: Portugal offers a diverse culinary scene that is worth exploring. From indulging in seafood delicacies in coastal regions to savouring hearty regional dishes in the countryside, there is something to please every palate. Visit local markets, traditional eateries, and food festivals to taste the authentic flavours of Portuguese cuisine.

2. Engage in Festivals and Traditions: Portugal is known for its lively festivals and cultural celebrations. From the Carnival parades to the religious processions and local fairs, there are numerous opportunities to immerse yourself in the vibrant Portuguese culture. Participate in these events, join in the festivities, and experience the unique traditions that bring communities together.

3. Visit Museums and Historical Sites: Portugal's rich history is reflected in its museums and historical landmarks. Explore iconic sites such as the Tower of Belém, Jerónimos Monastery, and the historical centres of Porto, Coimbra, and Évora. Discover the country's artistic heritage in museums like the Museu Nacional de Arte Antiga and engage with the local history through visits to

cultural sites.

4. Connect with Local Communities: Building connections with local communities is an excellent way to deepen your understanding of Portuguese culture. Engage with locals, join community groups or associations, and participate in cultural activities. This will provide you with opportunities to meet people, forge friendships, and gain insights into the authentic Portuguese way of life.

5. Stay Informed: Keep yourself updated on cultural events, exhibitions, and performances happening in your area. Leverage resources such as local event listings, city websites, and social media pages to stay informed about concerts, art shows, theatre performances, and other cultural happenings. This will allow you to make the most of the cultural offerings in your new surroundings.

6. Explore Lesser-Known Destinations: While popular cities like Lisbon and Porto offer a wealth of cultural experiences, don't forget to explore the lesser-known destinations. Venture off the beaten path and visit charming towns, villages, and natural landscapes that may offer unique cultural insights and a more authentic experience of Portuguese life.

7. Seek Cultural Resources: Portugal offers a wide range of cultural resources, including museums, libraries, and cultural centres. Take advantage of these institutions to explore art exhibitions, literary events, film screenings, and performances. The Calouste Gulbenkian Museum, the Museu Nacional de Arte Antiga, and the Casa da Música are just a few examples of cultural institutions to explore.

8. Connect with Expat Communities: Engaging with fellow expats can provide a sense of camaraderie and support as you navigate your new life in Portugal. Seek out expat communities, online forums, and social media groups where you can connect with others who have also chosen to embrace the Portuguese culture and lifestyle. Share experiences, tips, and recommendations to enhance your cultural journey.

By embracing the cultural treasures of Portugal, you will gain a deeper appreciation for the country's heritage, traditions, and way of life. Embrace the spirit of curiosity, openness, and respect as you explore the local cuisine, participate in festivals, and connect with the vibrant communities around you. Your willingness to engage with the culture will undoubtedly enrich your experience in this beautiful country.

5.1 Embracing the Culture and Lifestyle

Portugal is a country rich in traditions and festivities, with a calendar full of public and religious holidays throughout the year. These holidays offer a unique glimpse into the cultural fabric of the nation and provide opportunities to celebrate and engage with the local community. Here are some of the notable public and religious holidays in Portugal:

1. New Year's Day (Ano Novo) - January 1st: The start of the year is celebrated with fireworks, parties, and family gatherings.

2. Carnaval (Carnival) - February/March: This festive season precedes the Christian observance of Lent. It is a time of colorful parades, costumes, music, and dancing, with the cities of Lisbon, Torres Vedras, and Ovar being famous for their vibrant carnival celebrations.

3. Good Friday (Sexta-feira Santa) - Friday before Easter: The day commemorating the crucifixion of Jesus Christ is observed with religious processions and services.

4. Easter Sunday (Domingo de Páscoa) - Date varies: Easter Sunday marks the resurrection of Jesus Christ and is celebrated with church services, family gatherings, and traditional meals.

5. Liberty Day (Dia da Liberdade) - April 25th: This public holiday commemorates the Carnation Revolution of 1974, which ended the dictatorship in Portugal. It is celebrated with parades, concerts, and cultural events.

6. Labor Day (Dia do Trabalhador) - May 1st: A day to honor workers, with parades and demonstrations organized by labor unions.

7. Portugal Day (Dia de Portugal) - June 10th: This national holiday celebrates Portugal's cultural heritage, history, and achievements. Festivities include concerts, exhibitions, and traditional folklore performances.

8. Assumption Day (Assunção de Nossa Senhora) - August 15th: A religious holiday commemorating the Virgin Mary's assumption into heaven. It is observed with church services and processions.

9. Republic Day (Dia da República) - October 5th: The anniversary of the establishment of the Portuguese Republic in 1910. It is marked by official ceremonies, parades, and cultural events.

10. Christmas (Natal) - December 25th: The birth of Jesus Christ is celebrated with religious services, family gatherings, and the exchange of gifts.

In addition to these national holidays, various regional and local festivities take place throughout the year, showcasing unique cultural traditions and customs. These may include local patron saint celebrations, folklore festivals, and food fairs specific to different regions of Portugal.

It's important to note that during public holidays, some businesses, shops, and services may have limited hours or be closed. It can be an excellent opportunity to experience the local traditions, participate in festivities, and explore cultural events. Stay informed about holiday schedules and local customs by checking local event listings, city websites, or consulting with the local community.

Immerse yourself in the joyous atmosphere of Portuguese holidays, and embrace the opportunity to learn more about the country's cultural heritage, traditions, and religious practices. Celebrating these special occasions alongside the local community will provide you with memorable experiences and a deeper connection to the vibrant Portuguese culture.

5.2 Navigating Everyday Life:

Adjusting to the rhythm of everyday life in a new country can be an adventure in itself. In Portugal, embracing the local way of doing things will enhance your experience and help you integrate into the community. Here are some practical tips to navigate everyday life in Portugal:

1. Grocery Shopping: Familiarise yourself with local grocery stores and markets where you can find fresh produce, traditional Portuguese products, and international ingredients. Popular supermarket chains include Continente, Pingo Doce, and Lidl. Additionally, explore local markets such as Mercado da Ribeira in Lisbon or Mercado do Bolhão in Porto for a vibrant culinary experience.

2. Transportation: Portugal offers a reliable and efficient transportation system. In major cities like Lisbon and Porto, you can navigate the metro, buses, and trams. Consider purchasing a rechargeable public transportation card, such as the Lisboa Card or Porto Card, which provides discounted fares and access to multiple modes of transportation. If you prefer driving, familiarise yourself with local traffic rules and parking regulations.

Via Verde is an electronic toll collection system widely used in Portugal. It provides a convenient and efficient way for drivers to pay tolls on highways, bridges, and tunnels without the need to stop at toll booths. The system uses a small electronic device, called a Via Verde identifier, which is installed in the vehicle and automatically communicates with the tolling infrastructure as the vehicle passes through toll points.

With Via Verde, drivers can enjoy the benefits of seamless and faster travel, as they can pass through toll stations without having to queue or handle cash. The system is widely accepted across the country, including major highways and urban areas. Via Verde not only saves time but also eliminates the hassle of carrying loose change or searching for toll payment options.

To use Via Verde, drivers need to obtain a Via Verde identifier, which can be obtained at Via Verde stores, selected service areas, or through online registration. The device is linked to a prepaid account, and toll charges are automatically deducted each time a vehicle passes through a toll point.

Via Verde is not limited to toll payment services. It also offers additional features such as parking payments, fuel purchases at selected stations, and discounts at partner establishments. This multi-purpose functionality adds convenience to daily commuting and further enhances the overall experience of using Via Verde.

Whether you are a resident or a visitor in Portugal, utilizing Via Verde can streamline your journeys and make traveling more convenient. It is an efficient system that simplifies toll payments, allowing you to focus on enjoying the roads and exploring the beautiful landscapes of Portugal.

3. Healthcare Services: Portugal has a well-regarded healthcare system, both public and private. As a resident, you can access public healthcare services through the National Health Service (Serviço Nacional de Saúde - SNS) by registering with a local health center (Centro de Saúde). It is also advisable to have private health insurance to complement your healthcare needs. Research local hospitals, clinics, and doctors in your area, and keep important emergency contact numbers readily available.

4. Education: If you have children, you may be interested in understanding the education system in Portugal. Public schools offer free education to residents, and private and international schools provide alternative options. Research schools in your chosen area, consider the curriculum, language of instruction, and enrolment requirements. It's also worth connecting with local expat communities or online forums for advice and insights on schooling.

5. Cultural Etiquette: Familiarise yourself with Portuguese customs and cultural norms to navigate everyday interactions with ease. For example, greeting people with a handshake or kiss on

both cheeks is common in social settings. Embrace the relaxed pace of life, enjoy leisurely meals with family and friends, and savour the local cuisine.

To further assist you in navigating everyday life in Portugal, consider utilising the following resources:

- Online expat forums and social media groups: Connect with fellow expats and gain valuable insights from their experiences. Expat communities are often supportive and willing to share tips, advice, and local recommendations.

- Local city guides and websites: Consult local city guides, websites, and blogs that provide information on events, cultural activities, local services, and useful tips specific to your chosen city or region.

- Expat associations and organisations: Joining local expat associations or organisations can help you meet like-minded individuals, participate in cultural events, and access resources tailored to the needs of expatriates.

Embracing the everyday life in Portugal is an opportunity to immerse yourself in the local culture, build connections, and create a fulfilling experience in your new home. Stay open-minded, be curious, and embrace the beauty of everyday moments as you navigate your new life in Portugal.

6 "HOW TO"

How to Book Your Visa Interview at SEF or VFS Global

Once you have gathered all the necessary documents and are ready to proceed with your visa application, it's time to book your visa interview at either SEF (Serviço de Estrangeiros e Fronteiras) or VFS Global. Follow these steps to ensure a smooth process:

1. Determine the appropriate authority: Depending on the type of visa you are applying for, you may need to book your interview with SEF or VFS Global. SEF handles certain visa types directly, while others are processed through VFS Global, an outsourcing agency. Make sure to identify the correct authority based on your visa category.
https://www.sef.pt/en/Pages/homepage.aspx
https://www.vfsglobal.com/en/individuals/index.html

2. Gather required information: Before booking your visa interview, ensure you have all the necessary information at hand. This may include your passport details, visa application number, and any other relevant information provided during the application process.

3. Visit the official website: Go to the official website of SEF or VFS Global, depending on the authority you need to book your interview with. These websites provide comprehensive information

on visa application procedures, including how to schedule your appointment.

4. Navigate to the appointment booking section: Look for the section or tab on the website that allows you to schedule your visa interview. This may be labeled as "Appointment Booking" or "Visa Application Centre."

5. Select your location: Choose the appropriate location for your visa interview. Portugal may have multiple visa application centres or SEF offices, so ensure you select the one that is most convenient for you.

6. Check availability: Check the available dates and time slots for visa interviews. Some locations may have high demand, so it's advisable to book your appointment well in advance to secure your preferred date and time.

7. Fill in the required details: Provide the necessary information as prompted on the website. This may include personal details, contact information, passport details, and visa application details. Ensure the information you provide is accurate and matches the information provided in your visa application.

8. Choose the service type: Depending on the options available, you may have the choice of standard or priority processing. Select the service type that best suits your needs and budget.

9. Confirm your appointment: Once you have completed the required information, review your details for accuracy and confirm your appointment. Take note of any appointment reference or confirmation number provided.

10. Prepare supporting documents: Before your visa interview, ensure you have all the required supporting documents as outlined in the visa application guidelines. Organize them in a logical manner for easy presentation during the interview.

It's important to note that the specific steps and procedures for booking a visa interview may vary depending on the authority and location. Therefore, it's recommended to visit the official websites of SEF or VFS Global for detailed instructions and any updates regarding the visa application process.

By following these steps and preparing well in advance, you can secure your visa interview appointment and proceed with the next stages of your visa application process smoothly.

Checklist for Stage 1 interview

- Completed VFS form with 2 passport photos (blank form attached)
- Tax ID (NIF number) - you do not need a tax representative anymore to do this
- Proof of Portuguese bank statement (with a balance to show you can support yourself in Portugal)
- Proof of accommodation (long-term lease)
- Full Health Insurance (I wrote an affidavit saying I'd get insurance when I got here, I went with Medís when I arrived)
- Travel insurance (I printed off the free travel insurance I had with my UK Bank)
- Proof of passive income (e.g. rental income)
- 3 months' bank statements from home country
- Declaration why you want to live in Portugal
- Authorisation to do Portuguese criminal record check
- Your passport (and take a copy)
- UK Police Certificate - ACRO
- Fee to pay by card on the day of your appointment

You need to get your police certificate Apostilled. This takes a little time so if you book your appointment make sure you have time to get these things done.

Here is an online service https://www.hagueapostille.co.uk/

Here is an official checklist, please double check your own personal situation and requirements and ensure you are fully prepared for your interview.

https://imigrante.sef.pt/en/solicitar/residir/art77-1/

Stage 2 interview

When you arrive in Portugal with a D7 visa, there is often a second stage interview that takes place as part of the residency permit process. This interview is typically conducted by the Portuguese Immigration and Borders Service (SEF) and is aimed at assessing your compliance with the visa requirements (you do not need to speak Portuguese for this stage) Here are some details on what to expect during the second stage interview and a checklist to help you prepare:

1. Purpose of the interview: The second stage interview aims to verify your intentions and eligibility for the D7 visa, ensuring that you meet the requirements outlined by SEF.

2. Documentation: Gather all the necessary documents for the interview. This may include your passport, residence application form (submitted during the initial visa application), proof of financial means, health insurance coverage, proof of accommodation, and any other documents specified by SEF.

3. Review visa requirements: Familiarise yourself with the specific requirements of the D7 visa and ensure you meet them. This typically includes having a stable source of income or passive income, health insurance coverage, and suitable accommodation.

4. Prepare for questions: Anticipate potential questions during the interview. Be prepared to discuss your financial means, intention to reside in Portugal, purpose of the D7 visa, and your plans for integrating into Portuguese society.

5. Language proficiency: Although not mandatory, having a basic understanding of Portuguese can be beneficial during the interview. It demonstrates your commitment to integrating into the local culture and facilitates communication with the SEF officer.

6. Dress appropriately: Dress in formal or business attire for the interview to convey professionalism and respect.

7. Punctuality: Arrive on time for the interview. Being punctual demonstrates your commitment and respect for the process.

8. Stay calm and confident: Approach the interview with confidence and remain calm throughout. Answer questions truthfully and concisely, providing any requested information or documents promptly.

9. Checklist for the interview:
- Passport
- Residence application form
- Proof of financial means (bank statements, investment portfolios, or other supporting documents)
- Health insurance coverage proof
- Proof of accommodation (rental agreement, property ownership documents, etc.)
- Any additional documents specified by SEF

Remember to consult the SEF website or contact them directly for the most accurate and updated information regarding the second stage interview requirements for the D7 visa.

How to Obtain a Portuguese Bank Account

Opening a bank account in Portugal is an important step when relocating to the country. It allows you to manage your finances, receive payments, and carry out day-to-day banking transactions. Follow these instructions to obtain a Portuguese bank account:

1. Research and choose a bank: Start by researching different banks in Portugal. Consider factors such as their reputation, services offered, fees, and accessibility. Some popular banks in Portugal include Banco de Portugal, Caixa Geral de Depósitos, Millennium bcp, Santander Totta, and Novo Banco. It is advisable to choose a bank with a branch conveniently located near your residence or workplace.

2. Gather the required documents: Contact the bank you have chosen to inquire about the specific documents needed to open an account. Generally, you will need the following:

a. Valid identification: Bring your passport or national identity card. Make sure it is not expired.

b. Proof of address: Provide a document that confirms your residential address in Portugal, such as a rental contract or utility bill in your name.

c. Tax identification number (NIF): Obtain a Portuguese Tax Identification Number (Número de Identificação Fiscal or NIF) from the tax office (Serviço de Finanças) before opening a bank account. The NIF is a unique identifier required for various financial transactions in Portugal.

d. Proof of income or source of funds: Some banks may request proof of income, such as pay stubs or bank statements from your home country. They want to ensure that the source of your funds is legitimate.

3. Schedule an appointment: Contact the chosen bank to schedule an appointment to open a bank account. This will allow the bank staff to provide you with personalised assistance and ensure a smooth account opening process.

4. Visit the bank branch: On the scheduled date and time, visit the bank branch in person. Bring all the required documents and be prepared to fill out application forms.

5. Provide the necessary information: During your appointment, the bank representative will guide you through the account opening process. They will ask for your personal information, address, occupation, and other details as required. They may also explain the different types of accounts and services available, allowing you to choose the most suitable options.

6. Review terms and conditions: Take the time to review the terms and conditions of the bank account carefully. Ask any questions you may have to ensure you understand the fees, services, and policies associated with your account.

7. Complete the account opening process: Once all the necessary information is provided and the required forms are filled out, the bank will process your account opening request. They may provide you with an account number and any additional instructions or documents required.

8. Activate and access your account: Once your account is

successfully opened, the bank will provide you with details on how to activate and access your account. This may include information about online banking, ATM cards, and other banking facilities.

Suggested Banks in Portugal:

- Banco de Portugal
- Caixa Geral de Depósitos
- Millennium bcp
- Santander Totta
- Novo Banco

Please note that the specific requirements and procedures may vary slightly between different banks. It is advisable to contact your chosen bank directly or visit their official website for detailed information and any updates regarding the account opening process.

By following these instructions and providing all the necessary documents, you can successfully open a Portuguese bank account and start managing your finances in your new home.

In my personal experience, I opened a bank account in Lisbon with Millennium bcp and have nothing but an exceptional experience. When you read online, that's not everyone's experience and everyone has widely ranging views and opinions on banks. I was also allowed to use my UK address until such time as I could move to Portugal and change the address.

How to Obtain a Portuguese NIF (Número de Identificação Fiscal) Number

The Portuguese NIF, or Número de Identificação Fiscal, is a unique tax identification number required for various financial transactions and official purposes in Portugal. Here's a step-by-step guide on how to obtain a Portuguese NIF:

1. Determine the reason for obtaining an NIF: The process of obtaining an NIF may vary slightly depending on your purpose. The most common reasons for obtaining an NIF include employment, self-employment, starting a business, or purchasing

property. Identify the specific reason for obtaining the NIF as it will determine the documentation required.

2. Gather the necessary documents: Prepare the required documents based on your purpose for obtaining the NIF. The general documents needed include:

a. Passport or national identity card: Bring your valid passport or national identity card for identification purposes.

b. Proof of address: Provide a document that confirms your residential address in Portugal, such as a rental contract, utility bill, or bank statement in your name. (You don't necessarily have to have an address in Portugal, you can use a fiscal representative. Note that the date you change your fiscal address after you have moved to Portugal is the date you become a tax resident).

c. Supporting documents: Depending on your purpose, you may need additional documents. For example, if you're employed, you may need a work contract or an employment letter from your employer. If you're starting a business, you may need proof of business registration or relevant permits.

3. Visit the local tax office (Serviço de Finanças): Locate the nearest tax office (Serviço de Finanças) in your area. You can find the contact information and address of your local tax office on the website of the Portuguese Tax Authority (Autoridade Tributária e Aduaneira).

4. Schedule an appointment (optional): While it may not always be necessary, scheduling an appointment with the tax office can help ensure a smooth process. Contact the tax office beforehand to inquire if an appointment is required or recommended.

5. Complete the necessary forms: At the tax office, you will be provided with the appropriate forms to complete. These forms may vary depending on your purpose for obtaining the NIF. Fill out the forms accurately and provide all the required information.

6. Submit the required documents and forms: Present your identification documents, proof of address, and any other supporting documents requested by the tax office. Make sure to provide both the original documents and copies, as the tax office

may need to verify and retain the copies for their records.

7. Pay any applicable fees: Depending on the purpose of your NIF application, there may be fees involved. The tax office will inform you of any applicable fees and provide instructions on how to make the payment.

8. Receive your NIF: After submitting the necessary documents and paying any applicable fees, the tax office will process your application. If everything is in order, they will provide you with your Portuguese NIF. The NIF will be a unique identification number assigned to you for tax purposes.

Remember to keep your NIF number safe as you will need it for various official and financial transactions in Portugal, such as opening a bank account, signing contracts, or filing taxes.

It is advisable to contact the tax office or visit their official website for specific instructions and any updates regarding the NIF application process. Additionally, seeking assistance from a local expert or professional can provide valuable guidance during the application process.

Using a Fiscal Representative for your NIF number

When applying for a Portuguese NIF (Número de Identificação Fiscal), you have the option to use a fiscal representative to assist you with the application process. Here are some pieces of advice to consider when using a fiscal representative:

1. Choose a reputable fiscal representative: Research and choose a reliable fiscal representative who has experience and knowledge in assisting with NIF applications. Look for recommendations, reviews, or consult with expat communities or forums to find trusted professionals in the field.

2. Verify the fiscal representative's credentials: Ensure that the fiscal representative is registered and authorized to provide such services. Check their credentials, certifications, or affiliations with professional organizations related to taxation or legal services.

3. Understand the services provided: Discuss and clarify the scope of services offered by the fiscal representative. They can assist with various aspects of the NIF application process, such as completing forms, gathering required documents, and representing you before the tax authorities. Make sure you understand the specific services they will provide and any associated fees.

4. Provide necessary information and documents: Furnish the fiscal representative with all the relevant information and documents required for the NIF application. This includes your identification documents, proof of address, and any additional supporting documents based on your specific circumstances. Ensure that you provide accurate and up-to-date information to avoid any delays or complications.

5. Review the application before submission: Before the fiscal representative submits your NIF application, review all the details provided. Double-check that the information is accurate and matches your documents. If you have any concerns or questions, address them with the fiscal representative before proceeding.

6. Stay informed and engaged: While the fiscal representative will handle the application process on your behalf, it's important to stay informed and engaged. Ask questions, seek updates on the progress of your application, and maintain open communication with the fiscal representative. This will help ensure that you are aware of the process and any additional requirements or steps that may arise.

7. Retain copies of all documents: Keep copies of all the documents submitted through the fiscal representative. It's essential to have a record of your application and supporting documents for future reference or any potential inquiries from authorities.

8. Seek advice from multiple sources: Using a fiscal representative can be beneficial, but it's also wise to seek advice from multiple sources. Consult with professionals in the field, such as tax advisors or lawyers, to ensure you have a comprehensive understanding of the NIF application process and its implications.

Remember, using a fiscal representative is an optional choice, and you can choose to apply for the NIF directly without assistance. Assess your personal circumstances, needs, and comfort level before deciding whether to engage a fiscal representative for your NIF application.

I have heard of people paying €180 to €1,800 for this service, personally I didn't realise when I was applying that I could have done it myself. I paid a lawyer to do it for me costing €680. And then they held my password random as they wouldn't change the address after I'd moved without additional fees. They also said that the service automatically renewed so I had a surprise invoice in year 2 for another €680 which I fought and had cancelled. I'm sharing this so you can go in with your eyes wide open.

How to change your NIF address to Portugal on Finanças portal

To change your NIF (Número de Identificação Fiscal) address to Portugal on the Finanças portal, follow these steps:

1. Log in to your Finanças portal: Access your personal account on the Finanças portal using your username and password.

2. Navigate to the "Dados Pessoais" (Personal Data) section: Once logged in, look for a section called "Dados Pessoais" or "Personal Data." This section typically contains options to update your personal information.

3. Select the option to update your address: Within the "Dados Pessoais" section, you should find an option to update your address. This may be labeled as "Atualizar Morada" or a similar term.

4. Provide the new address details: Fill in the required fields with your new address in Portugal. Include the street name, house number, postal code, city, and any other relevant information. Make sure to provide accurate and complete information.

5. Save the changes: After entering the new address details, review the information to ensure its accuracy. Then, save the changes by clicking on the appropriate button or link provided on

the portal.

6. Verify the address change: Once the changes are saved, the portal may prompt you to verify the new address. This could involve receiving a verification code or confirmation letter at your new address. Follow the instructions provided to complete the verification process.

7. Confirm the address change: After verifying the new address, you may need to confirm the address change within the Finanças portal. This step may vary depending on the specific requirements and procedures of the portal.

It's important to keep your address updated on the Finanças portal to ensure that any official communications or documents are sent to your correct address in Portugal. If you encounter any difficulties or have specific questions regarding the address change process on the Finanças portal, it is recommended to reach out to the tax authorities or consult a tax advisor for assistance.

To apply for Non-Habitual Resident (NHR) status in Portugal

1. Understand the NHR program: Familiarise yourself with the requirements, benefits, and eligibility criteria of the NHR program. The NHR status aims to attract foreign residents with high-value skills and promote tax benefits for a specific period.

2. Consult a tax advisor: Seek guidance from a qualified tax advisor or specialist who can provide personalised advice based on your individual circumstances and help you navigate the application process. (There are reputable consultants with whom you can book a one hour consultation to discuss your particular situation and to understand the steps.)*

3. Gather necessary documentation: Prepare the required documents, which typically include:
- Proof of residency in Portugal
- Identification documents (passport, ID card, etc.)
- Tax identification number (NIF)
- Proof of income and tax returns from previous countries of

residence

    - Employment contracts or proof of self-employment, if applicable

4. Submit the application: Contact the Portuguese tax authorities (Autoridade Tributária e Aduaneira) or consult a tax advisor to submit your NHR application. The application process typically involves completing specific forms and providing the necessary supporting documents.

5. Await the decision: The tax authorities will review your application and assess your eligibility for NHR status. The processing time can vary, but it usually takes a few weeks to a few months to receive a decision.

6. Notification of NHR status: Once your application is approved, you will receive notification of your NHR status. This status entitles you to the tax benefits and advantages associated with the program.

It's worth noting that the application for NHR status should be made within the first six months of becoming a tax resident in Portugal. Therefore, it is important to initiate the process promptly after relocating to Portugal.

To ensure accuracy and compliance with the NHR program requirements, it is recommended to seek professional advice from a tax advisor or consult the relevant authorities for the most up-to-date information and specific time frames for making your NHR application.

*You do not need to pay someone to make your NHR application. I was quoted €800 for a consultant to do it for me and when I realised that if you have access to your online Financias portal you can do it yourself and it's a matter of ticking a box I was fuming.

If you have access to your online Finanças portal in Portugal, you can apply for Non-Habitual Resident (NHR) status through the following steps (please note that you need to have updated your NIF address to your Portugal address in order to apply for NHR)

1. Log in to your Finanças portal: Access your personal account on the Finanças portal using your username and password.

2. Navigate to the NHR section: Once logged in, navigate to the section dedicated to Non-Habitual Residents or any relevant tax category related to NHR. This section may be labeled as "Residentes Não Habituais" or "Regime Fiscal para Residentes Não Habituais."

3. Complete the application form: Fill out the application form provided on the online portal. The form will typically ask for personal information, details about your previous tax residency, and supporting documents.

4. Upload the required documents: Prepare and upload the necessary supporting documents to accompany your application. These documents may include proof of residency, identification documents, tax returns from previous countries of residence, and any other documents specific to your situation.

5. Review and submit the application: Carefully review the information you have provided and ensure that all the required fields are accurately filled. Once you are confident that the application is complete, submit it through the online portal.

6. Await the decision: The tax authorities will review your application and assess your eligibility for NHR status. The processing time may vary, but you can monitor the status of your application through your Finanças portal or contact the tax authorities for updates.

While applying for NHR status through the online Finanças portal can be convenient, it is still advisable to consult a tax advisor or specialist to ensure that you meet all the requirements and provide accurate information. They can also assist you in navigating the online application process and address any specific questions or concerns you may have.

How to obtain a Utente number

To obtain a Utente number in Portugal, which is necessary for accessing healthcare services, follow these steps:

1. Register with the Portuguese National Health Service (SNS): Visit your local health centre or Centro de Saúde to register with the SNS. You will need to provide your identification document (passport or residence card) and proof of address.

2. Complete the registration form: Fill out the registration form provided by the health centre. The form will require personal information such as your full name, date of birth, contact details, and any relevant medical history.

3. Obtain a health user card: After completing the registration form, you will receive a health user card (Cartão de Utente). This card serves as proof of your registration with the SNS and your Utente number. Keep this card in a safe place as you will need it when accessing healthcare services.

4. Choose a primary care doctor: During the registration process, you may be asked to select a primary care doctor or Médico de Família. This doctor will be your main point of contact for general healthcare needs and referrals to specialists.

5. Keep your information up to date: It is essential to inform the health centre of any changes to your personal information, such as address or contact details. This will ensure that your records are accurate and up to date.

6. Accessing healthcare services: With your Utente number and health user card, you can now access healthcare services within the Portuguese National Health Service. When visiting a healthcare facility, present your health user card to check in and receive appropriate care.

It's important to note that the process for obtaining a Utente number may vary slightly depending on your specific circumstances and the region where you reside. It is recommended to contact your local health centre or SNS office for precise instructions and any additional requirements.

Remember to carry your health user card with you when seeking medical assistance, as it will be necessary to access healthcare services and receive appropriate treatment.

How to obtain a NISS number

In Portugal, a Social Security number, known as "Número de Identificação da Segurança Social" or NISS, is required for various purposes, including employment, accessing social benefits, and contributing to the social security system. Here's when you may need a Social Security number and how to obtain one:

1. Employment: If you plan to work in Portugal, you will need a Social Security number. Your employer will require this number to ensure proper social security contributions are made on your behalf.

2. Accessing Social Benefits: To access social benefits such as unemployment benefits, healthcare, maternity/paternity benefits, or retirement pensions, you will need a Social Security number.

3. Self-Employment: If you plan to start your own business or work as a freelancer in Portugal, you will need a Social Security number to register as self-employed and make contributions to the social security system.

To obtain a Social Security number in Portugal, follow these steps:

1. Visit the Social Security office (Segurança Social): Locate the nearest Social Security office in your area. You can find the office addresses and contact information on the website of the Portuguese Social Security Institute (Instituto da Segurança Social).

2. Gather necessary documents: Prepare the required documents, which may include your passport or residence permit, proof of address, and any other relevant identification documents.

3. Submit your application: Visit the Social Security office in

person and complete the application form for a Social Security number. Provide all the necessary documents along with the completed form.

4. Verification and issuance: The Social Security office will verify your application and supporting documents. If everything is in order, they will assign you a Social Security number and issue a NISS card.

It's important to note that the specific requirements and procedures may vary depending on your individual circumstances, such as your residency status and employment situation. It is advisable to contact the Social Security office or consult their official website for detailed information and guidance specific to your situation.

Obtaining a Social Security number is a crucial step for accessing various benefits and services in Portugal. Make sure to keep your NISS card in a safe place, as you may be required to present it in various official and employment-related situations.

How to change your driving licence to a Portuguese driving licence

When you arrive in Portugal to live, you have a limited timeframe to change your UK or USA driving licence to a Portuguese driving licence. The specific rules and requirements may vary, so it's important to consult the Portuguese authorities and relevant websites for the most up-to-date information. However, here are the general steps involved:

1. Determine the time limit: As a resident of Portugal, you are typically given a limited period, usually 90 days, to register your foreign driving licence for a Portuguese one. It's important to check the specific time limit applicable to your situation.

2. Gather necessary documents: Before heading to the driver's licence authority, gather the required documents. This usually includes your original driving licence, proof of residence in Portugal, proof of identity (passport or ID card), a passport-sized photo, and any other specific documents requested by the

authorities.

3. Schedule an appointment: In Portugal, the driver's licence exchange process is typically handled by the Instituto da Mobilidade e dos Transportes (IMT). Visit their website or contact them directly to schedule an appointment at a local IMT office.

4. Attend the appointment: On the scheduled day, visit the designated IMT office at the appointed time. Bring all the necessary documents with you.

5. Submit the application: At the IMT office, complete the application form for exchanging your driving licence. Present your original driving licence, supporting documents, and the completed application form to the authorities.

6. Undergo any necessary tests: Depending on the specific circumstances and the country of origin of your driving licence, you may need to undergo certain tests, such as a medical examination or a driving test. The authorities will inform you if any additional tests are required.

7. Pay the applicable fees: There may be fees associated with exchanging your driving licence. Ensure you have the necessary funds to cover the costs, which can vary depending on the circumstances.

8. Await the new driving licence: After completing the necessary steps and providing all the required documents, you will be informed about the status of your application. Once approved, you will receive your Portuguese driving licence.

Remember to consult the official website of the IMT or relevant driving licence authority in Portugal for the most accurate and up-to-date information. They can provide specific details on the documents required, fees, and any additional steps involved in changing your UK or USA driving licence to a Portuguese one.

How to change address on your residency card

When you have a temporary residency card in Portugal and you move to a new address, it is important to update your address with the relevant authorities. Here is a step-by-step guide on how to change your address:

1. Visit the local town hall (Câmara Municipal) or the Citizen's Shop (Loja do Cidadão): These are the primary locations where you can update your address information. Locate the nearest town hall or Citizen's Shop in your new area of residence.

2. Prepare the necessary documents: Gather the required documents for changing your address. These may include:
   - Your temporary residency card (cartão de residência)
   - Proof of your new address, such as a rental agreement or a utility bill in your name

3. Visit the local town hall or Citizen's Shop: Go to the designated office during their working hours. Take the necessary documents with you.

4. Inform the staff: Inform the staff that you would like to update your address. They will provide you with the appropriate forms to fill out.

5. Complete the forms: Fill out the forms with your updated address information. Provide any additional details or documents requested.

6. Submit the documents: Hand in the completed forms and the required documents to the staff. They will process your request.

7. Receive confirmation: Once your address change is processed, you will receive confirmation of the update. This may be in the form of a document or a stamp on your temporary residency card.

8. Update other relevant authorities: Inform other entities about your change of address, such as your bank, utility providers, healthcare providers, and any other organizations or institutions that need your updated address.

It is important to complete the address change process

promptly after moving to your new residence to ensure that your information is up to date with the authorities. This helps ensure smooth communication and avoids any potential issues with official documentation.

Please note that the specific process may vary slightly depending on the municipality or region in which you reside. It is advisable to consult the local town hall or Citizen's Shop for precise instructions and any additional requirements specific to your area.

Updating your will after you move to Portugal

If you had a will in your home country and have moved to Portugal, it is advisable to review and update your will to ensure its validity and effectiveness in Portugal. While the specifics of updating a will may vary depending on your individual circumstances, here are some general steps to consider:

1. Consult with a legal professional: Seek advice from a qualified lawyer or notary in Portugal who specialises in estate planning and wills. They can guide you through the process and provide tailored recommendations based on your specific situation.

2. Understand Portuguese inheritance laws: Familiarise yourself with the inheritance laws and regulations in Portugal, as they may differ from those in your home country. Understanding these laws will help ensure that your will complies with local requirements.

3. Translation and notarisation: If your existing will is written in a language other than Portuguese, you may need to have it translated into Portuguese. Additionally, you may need to have the translated will notarised or authenticated by a competent authority.

4. Seek legal advice on the validity of the existing will: Consult with a legal professional to determine if your existing will is recognised and enforceable in Portugal. They can assess its validity and advise you on any necessary changes or amendments to make it compliant with Portuguese laws.

5. Consider a new will in Portugal: Depending on the

complexity of your situation and the differences between your home country's laws and Portuguese laws, it may be advisable to create a new will specifically for your assets and circumstances in Portugal. This new will can be tailored to meet the legal requirements and address your specific wishes under Portuguese law.

6. Update beneficiaries and asset distribution: Review and update the beneficiaries and asset distribution in your will to reflect any changes in your personal circumstances or preferences since your relocation to Portugal. Ensure that your will clearly outlines how your assets should be distributed upon your passing, taking into account any applicable Portuguese inheritance laws.

7. Seek professional advice on tax implications: Estate and inheritance tax laws vary between countries. Consult with a tax advisor or estate planning expert who can provide guidance on any tax implications that may arise from updating your will for Portugal.

It is crucial to consult with a legal professional who is knowledgeable about both the laws of your home country and those of Portugal. They can guide you through the process of updating your will, ensuring that it aligns with the requirements of Portuguese law and provides appropriate protection for your assets and beneficiaries in Portugal.

How to import a car to Portugal

Importing a car to Portugal is a process that involves specific requirements and procedures. Here are the key points to consider when importing a car:

1. Residency Status: To import a car to Portugal, you typically need to be a resident of the country. Non-residents may also import a car, but the process and requirements may differ.

2. Age and Origin of the Car: Portugal has specific regulations regarding the importation of cars based on their age and origin. Generally, cars manufactured within the European Union (EU) can be imported without significant restrictions, while cars from

outside the EU may be subject to additional requirements.

3. Vehicle Documentation: You will need to gather and prepare the necessary documentation for the importation process. This usually includes the vehicle's original registration certificate, purchase invoice, proof of ownership, and any other relevant documents related to the vehicle's history and condition.

4. Customs Clearance: Upon arrival in Portugal, the vehicle must go through customs clearance procedures. This involves declaring the car and paying any applicable customs duties and taxes, such as import duties and value-added tax (VAT). The customs authorities will provide you with the necessary forms and guidance.

5. Technical Inspection and Homologation: Imported cars must undergo a technical inspection and homologation process to ensure compliance with Portuguese safety and environmental standards. This involves obtaining a Portuguese conformity certificate (Certificado de Conformidade) or equivalent documentation from the manufacturer.

6. Registration and Licensing: Once the car meets all the necessary requirements, you can proceed with its registration and licensing in Portugal. This includes obtaining a Portuguese license plate, paying registration fees, and completing the necessary paperwork at the local vehicle registration office (Instituto da Mobilidade e dos Transportes - IMT).

7. Import Taxes and Fees: Importing a car to Portugal may be subject to various taxes and fees, including customs duties, VAT, and the Vehicle Tax (Imposto Único de Circulação - IUC). It's important to research and understand the applicable taxes and fees beforehand to properly budget for the importation process.

To ensure a smooth and successful importation process, it is recommended to seek professional advice from a customs agent or a specialised company experienced in vehicle importation. They can guide you through the specific requirements, paperwork, and procedures involved in importing a car to Portugal, as well as assist with customs clearance and related matters. Additionally, it's advisable to consult the Portuguese Customs website (Autoridade Tributária e Aduaneira) or contact the nearest Portuguese consulate for detailed and up-to-date information regarding car importation regulations and procedures.

Portuguese tax year and tax dates to take note of

In Portugal, the tax year follows the calendar year, running from January 1st to December 31st. It's important to be aware of the following key tax-related dates and deadlines:

1. Income Tax Return Filing:
   - Individuals: The deadline for filing the personal income tax return (Modelo 3) for most individuals is typically between April 1st and June 30th of the following year. However, specific deadlines may vary, so it's advisable to check with the tax authorities or consult with a tax professional to confirm the exact dates for each tax year.
   - Self-employed Individuals: Self-employed individuals must file their income tax return by May 31st of the following year.

2. Payment of Taxes:
   - Income Tax: The payment of income tax is generally done in three instalments: the first in April, the second in July, and the final instalment in September. The exact dates may vary each year, so it's important to check the specific deadlines announced by the tax authorities.

3. Value Added Tax (VAT):
   - VAT returns and payments are typically due on a quarterly basis, with the following deadlines: April 10th (for the 1st quarter), July 10th (for the 2nd quarter), October 10th (for the 3rd quarter), and January 10th (for the 4th quarter).

4. Property Tax (IMI):
   - The payment of the property tax (IMI) is usually due in two installments. The first installment is typically due by the end of April, and the second installment is due by the end of November. However, it's important to note that these deadlines can vary, and you should consult the specific deadlines announced by the tax authorities each year.

5. Other Taxes:

- Various other taxes, such as Corporate Income Tax, Capital Gains Tax, and Stamp Duty, have their own specific deadlines depending on the nature of the tax and the taxpayer involved. These deadlines can vary and may depend on factors such as the legal form of the entity and the specific circumstances of the taxpayer. It's advisable to consult with a tax professional or the tax authorities to ensure compliance with the relevant deadlines.

It's crucial to stay informed about any changes or updates to the tax year dates and deadlines, as these can be subject to amendments by the Portuguese tax authorities. It's recommended to consult official sources, such as the Portuguese tax authority website (Autoridade Tributária e Aduaneira), or seek advice from a tax professional for the most accurate and up-to-date information regarding tax year dates and deadlines in Portugal.

Tips for navigating this information overload and overwhelm

1. There are going to be dozens of websites you reference, websites that you need to login to. I suggest you make a bookmarks folder on your web browser and keep them all to hand. This will save loads of time and keep everything you need in one place.

2. Create a separate email account for your life in Portugal. Having everything to do with your VISA applications, accounts, websites on one email address will make life a whole lot easier. You can create folders in that email account to keep things separate relating to your visa, your housing, bills, taxes and so on.

3. Create a note on your phone to keep your NIF number, your full address and a few key phrases that will help you in Portuguese. Having this to hand will save you loads of time when you're asked for your NIF or you need your full address and can't remember it or pronounce it properly. Of course please keep your data secure.

4. Save the phone numbers of local authorities, police, ambulance in your phone, embassy. It'll be different to your home country and you'll never know when you need it.

5. Keep a photo album or file on your phone and take pictures of your Passport, residency card, proof of address, driving licence etc. It's not mandatory to carry identification with you at all times but having access to it can be helpful. Make sure your folders are password protected as that is highly sensitive personally identifiable information.

6. For energy suppliers to getting notifications and ordering pizza you're going to need a Portuguese mobile number. You can set up a virtual sim so you can have your home number continuing to run and a Portuguese number on your phone at the same time. Remember your current number will have all your 2FA set up so give yourself time before you switch off your old number. Don't wait too long before your home network carrier starts implementing high roaming charges.

7 MOVING TO PORTUGAL WITH PETS

7.1 Understanding the Requirements and Process

Moving to Portugal with your furry companions requires careful planning and adherence to certain requirements. In this chapter, we will guide you through the process of relocating your pets, ensuring their safety and compliance with Portuguese regulations. From understanding the necessary documentation to preparing for travel, we will provide you with essential information to make the transition as smooth as possible.

7.2 Researching Pet Import Requirements

Before making the move, it's crucial to research and understand the pet import requirements specific to Portugal. Each country has its own regulations regarding pet importation, including vaccinations, health certificates, and microchipping. Check the official website of the Direção-Geral de Alimentação e Veterinária (DGAV) or consult with your local veterinary authorities for up-to-date information on the specific requirements for bringing pets into Portugal.

7.3 Veterinary Health Check and Vaccinations

Ensure that your pets are in good health and up to date with their vaccinations before traveling to Portugal. Schedule a visit to your veterinarian well in advance to conduct a thorough health check and ensure all necessary vaccinations, including rabies, are up to date. The veterinarian will issue a pet health certificate, which is typically required for international travel.

7.4 Microchipping and Identification

Microchipping your pets is a mandatory requirement in many countries, including Portugal. Make sure your pets are microchipped with an ISO-compliant microchip before the move. It's essential to update the microchip information with your current contact details, including your Portuguese address and contact number.

7.5 Applying for an EU Pet Passport

The EU Pet Passport is an official document that allows for easy travel within the European Union with your pets. Contact your veterinarian to obtain an EU Pet Passport for each of your pets. The passport will contain their identification information, vaccination records, and other relevant details. The EU Pet Passport simplifies the process of traveling with your pets within the EU.

If you are in the UK, due to Brexit you can no longer obtain an EU pet passport. Your veterinarian will prepare an Animal Health Certificate. It's valid for 10 days for entry to the EU so you need to book the appointment with your vet when you know your travel arrangements. Here is more information on taking your pet abroad to an EU country.

7.7 Transportation and Travel Arrangements

When making travel arrangements for your pets, consider the most suitable mode of transportation. If you're flying to Portugal, check with airlines about their pet policies and requirements. Some airlines allow pets to travel in the cabin with you, while others may require them to be transported as cargo. Ensure that you comply with all airline regulations and book your pet's travel well in advance.

7.7 Pet-Friendly Accommodation

When searching for accommodation in Portugal, consider the needs of your pets. Look for pet-friendly housing options that allow animals and provide a safe and comfortable environment. Some landlords or rental properties may have specific policies or restrictions regarding pets, so it's important to inquire about these details before signing a lease agreement.

7.8 Settling in and Local Pet Services

Once you arrive in Portugal, familiarise yourself with the local pet services available in your area. Find a reputable veterinarian who can provide routine care, emergency services, and any necessary follow-up vaccinations or treatments. Additionally, explore local pet stores, groomers, and pet-friendly parks or walking trails to ensure your pets can enjoy a happy and healthy life in their new surroundings.

Moving to Portugal with your pets requires careful planning and attention to detail. By understanding the import requirements, ensuring your pets' health and identification, and making appropriate travel arrangements, you can ensure a safe and comfortable transition for your beloved companions. Always stay informed and consult with the relevant authorities to ensure compliance with regulations and provide the best possible care for your pets throughout the process.

7.9 Protecting Your Pets from Hazards in Portugal

While Portugal offers a wonderful environment for pets, it's important to be aware of potential dangers that can affect their well-being. One significant hazard to be cautious of in Portugal is the presence of processionary caterpillars. These caterpillars are known for their toxic hairs, which can cause severe reactions if touched or ingested by pets. Keep a close eye on your pets during the warmer months, especially in areas with pine trees where processionary caterpillars are commonly found. If you suspect your pet has come into contact with these caterpillars or is displaying unusual symptoms such as excessive drooling, vomiting, or difficulty breathing, seek immediate veterinary assistance.

In addition to processionary caterpillars, there are other potential hazards that can affect dogs and cats in Portugal. Some plants, such as oleander and azalea, can be toxic if ingested by pets. It's important to familiarise yourself with the common poisonous plants in the region and ensure they are not accessible to your pets.

Portugal also has its share of common pests, including ticks and mosquitoes. These pests can transmit diseases to pets, such as Lyme disease and heart worm. Take preventive measures by regularly checking your pets for ticks, using tick repellents, and discussing appropriate preventative treatments with your veterinarian.

Furthermore, be mindful of the heat during the summer months, as Portugal can experience high temperatures. Dogs, in particular, are susceptible to heatstroke. Provide plenty of fresh water, avoid walking dogs during the hottest times of the day, and never leave pets unattended in a parked car, as temperatures can quickly become life-threatening. Many beaches don't allow dogs however, if you do find yourself on the beach please be very mindful of baited fishing hooks that are often left behind. Unfortunately vets in Portugal are very experienced at removing fishing hooks from the stomachs of dogs!

To ensure the well-being of your pets, it's recommended to consult with a local veterinarian who can provide guidance on local hazards, preventive measures, and treatments. They can also advise on suitable products for parasite control and offer recommendations specific to your pet's needs.

By being aware of these potential hazards and taking proactive steps to protect your pets, you can provide a safe and enjoyable environment for them to thrive in Portugal. Stay vigilant, keep an eye on your surroundings, and seek professional advice whenever necessary to ensure your furry friends are safe and healthy throughout your time in Portugal.

7.10 Personal accounts of travelling with dogs

When we arrived in Portugal, we flew from London to Lisbon on TAP. As our dogs were under 8 kgs they flew in the cabin with us.

It's one dog per passenger and the pet ticket adds anything from €70 to €180 depending on your flight.

Your dogs need to be in an airline approved travel crate (you can find plenty on amazon). Upon arrival at Heathrow they did check the weight and made sure the dogs were comfortable. Checkin was easy and the dogs got lots of attention at the airport.

The airline you're flying with will have information on the ticket, travel crate and requirements. (Here's a link to TAP Travelling with Animals).

Before departing, we filled in the forms to notify Lisbon airport of the arrival and pre-paid the veterinary check fee. We had all their paperwork sent over beforehand but made sure I had copies to hand on arrival. This made things really easy when we landed, we found the vet office near the carousels, had our documents stamped and we were on our way in minutes. (You can find the forms and details here).

Overall it was a good experience, the dogs did great and we didn't have any issues. This isn't everyone's experience but if you plan ahead you can make it easier for you and your furry friends.

8 PORTUGUESE PROPERTY MARKET

The Portuguese property market has experienced significant growth in recent years, attracting both domestic and international buyers. However, it's essential to navigate this market with caution and be aware of potential pitfalls and challenges. In this chapter, we will explore the state of the Portuguese property market, discussing its opportunities, overpricing concerns, excess properties, and provide references to articles, research, and statistics to support our analysis.

1. Market Opportunities:

The Portuguese property market has been a popular choice for investors and homebuyers due to various factors. These include affordable property prices compared to other European countries, a favourable climate, attractive lifestyle, and government initiatives to encourage foreign investment, such as the Golden Visa program. Additionally, regions like Lisbon, Porto, and the Algarve have witnessed significant development and increased demand, offering opportunities for property appreciation and rental income.

2. Overpricing Concerns:

While the Portuguese property market presents opportunities, overpricing can be a concern in certain areas. In popular tourist destinations or prime city locations, there might be instances of inflated property prices due to high demand. It's crucial for buyers to conduct thorough research, seek professional advice, and compare prices in the market to avoid overpaying. Consulting local real estate agents, engaging in property appraisals, and reviewing market trends can help buyers make informed decisions.

There is a stress on the pricing bubble, even though if you suggest that in conversation you'll likely be shot down. I'd like to direct you to this YouTube video talking about the Housing Sales Crash before you buy.

3. Excess Properties:

Another aspect of the Portuguese property market is the existence of excess properties, particularly in certain regions and segments. The global financial crisis and subsequent economic challenges resulted in a surplus of properties, including bank repossessions and unfinished developments. While this situation has improved in recent years, buyers should still exercise caution and conduct due diligence to ensure they are investing in viable and legally sound properties.

References:

1. According to a report by Confidencial Imobiliário, Portugal's property market experienced a 15.5% year-on-year increase in house prices in 2021. [Source: "Portuguese property market breaks records despite pandemic" - Portugal Resident, 2022]

2. An article by The Guardian highlights the growing concern of overpricing in Lisbon's property market, driven by high demand from foreign investors. [Source: "Lisbon's property market is booming, but locals are getting left out" - The Guardian, 2021]

3. The National Institute of Statistics (Instituto Nacional de Estatística - INE) provides comprehensive data and reports on the Portuguese property market, including housing prices, sales, and market trends. [Website: INE Portugal]

Navigating the Portuguese property market requires a balance of careful research, professional guidance, and understanding of market dynamics. By being well-informed about current trends, pricing patterns, and potential challenges, buyers can make more informed decisions and avoid common pitfalls. It is recommended to consult local real estate professionals, stay updated on market news and reports, and conduct thorough due diligence before making any property purchase in Portugal.

9 EXPLORING THE REALITIES

While Portugal offers numerous advantages and a high quality of life, it's important to acknowledge and address some of the downsides or potential challenges you may encounter when moving to the country. It is essential to approach your new life in Portugal with realistic expectations and an understanding of the local dynamics. Let's explore some of the common concerns that expatriates may face:

1. Perception of entitlement: As a foreigner in Portugal, you may encounter instances where you are labeled as an entitled foreigner (some foreigners may be entitled as things here don't work the way they do in your home country). Some locals may hold the perception that foreigners drive up prices, particularly in the housing market, and contribute to the gentrification of certain areas. It is important to be respectful and aware of local sensitivities, actively engage with the community, and contribute positively to your new surroundings.

2. Language barrier: Although many Portuguese people speak English, especially in tourist areas, the language barrier can still pose challenges in certain situations. Communicating in Portuguese can be beneficial for day-to-day interactions, building relationships, and navigating administrative processes. Learning the basics of the Portuguese language can help you integrate more easily into the local community and enhance your overall experience.

3. Bureaucratic procedures: Portugal, like any other country, has its fair share of bureaucratic procedures, which can sometimes be time-consuming and complex. Obtaining residency permits, dealing with government agencies, or understanding tax regulations may require patience and perseverance. Seeking guidance from professionals or expat communities can help you navigate these processes more smoothly.

4. Housing affordability: In popular areas, such as Lisbon and Porto, there has been an increase in property prices, leading to affordability challenges for both locals and expatriates. The demand for housing has outpaced supply in some regions, creating a housing shortage. It's important to research the housing market thoroughly, explore different areas, and consider alternative locations that offer more affordable options.

5. Cultural differences: Moving to a new country means encountering different cultural norms and practices. Some expatriates may initially find it challenging to adapt to the local customs, work culture, or social dynamics. However, with an open mind, curiosity, and willingness to learn, you can embrace the cultural differences, build relationships, and integrate into the Portuguese way of life.

It is essential to recognise that while there may be challenges, moving to Portugal also brings numerous benefits and positive contributions to the country. Expatriates can play a vital role in Portugal's economic growth, cultural diversity, and social fabric. Some of the benefits that expatriates bring include:

1. Economic growth: Expatriates contribute to Portugal's economy through job creation, entrepreneurship, and investments. They bring diverse skills, knowledge, and expertise that can drive innovation and enhance various industries.

2. Cultural exchange: Expatriates enrich Portugal's cultural landscape by sharing their own traditions, perspectives, and experiences. This cultural exchange fosters diversity, understanding, and the formation of global communities within the country.

3. Tourism boost: Expatriates often promote Portugal as a destination of choice, attracting more tourists and boosting the tourism industry. Their firsthand experiences and positive recommendations contribute to the growth of this vital sector.

4. Social integration: Expatriates actively engage with local communities, participating in social initiatives, and contributing to the overall well-being of Portuguese society. This interaction fosters integration, understanding, and the building of harmonious relationships between locals and expatriates.

In conclusion, while it is important to acknowledge the downsides or challenges that may arise when moving to Portugal, it is equally crucial to recognise the positive contributions and benefits that expatriates bring to the country. It's important to adopt and attitude of being a part of the solution and not contributing to the problems.

10 USEFUL RESOURCES

Here is a collated list of useful websites, resources, and YouTube channels to help you navigate life in Portugal. Please note that I am in no way affiliated with the following and by including these links they are a resource and reference only and not a recommendation.

Websites:

Visit Portugal (www.visitportugal.com) - Official website of Turismo de Portugal with information on tourism, culture, and events.

Expat.com (www.expat.com/portugal) - Online community and resource platform for expatriates in Portugal, offering forums, guides, and classifieds.

Expatica Portugal (www.expatica.com/pt) - News, information, and guides for expats in Portugal, covering various aspects of life in the country.

Angloinfo Portugal (www.angloinfo.com/portugal) - Comprehensive information and resources for English-speaking expats in Portugal.

Official websites

Serviço de Estrangeiros e Fronteiras (SEF) (www.sef.pt) - Official website of the Portuguese Immigration and Borders Service, providing information on visas, residence permits, and immigration procedures.

VFS Global (VFS) (https://www.vfsglobal.com/en/individuals/index.html) - website for information on visas, evisas, permits and centres to apply for entry.

AT Autoridad tributária e aduaneira (Finanças) (https://www.portaldasfinancas.gov.pt/at/html/index.html) - financial portal for tax services.

Resources:

Living in Portugal Guide (https://www.gov.uk/guidance/living-in-portugal) A detailed guidebook for British Citizens moving to or living in Portugal.

"The Rough Guide to Portugal" - A travel guidebook offering insights into Portuguese culture, history, and practical information for travellers and residents. (https://www.amazon.com/Rough-Guide-Portugal-Guides/dp/0241253918)

"Portugal Confidential" (www.portugalconfidential.com) - Online magazine featuring articles, reviews, and recommendations on Portuguese culture, gastronomy, and lifestyle.

EasyExpat Portugal (www.easyexpat.com/en/guides/portugal.htm) - Expat guides covering various aspects of living in Portugal, including housing, healthcare, education, and more.

Internations Portugal (www.internations.org/portugal-expats/guide) - An online community and resource platform for expatriates, providing information, forums, and networking opportunities.

YouTube Channels:

Portugalist (www.youtube.com/c/Portugalist) - A YouTube channel dedicated to all things Portugal, including travel tips, cultural insights, and expat experiences.

Expats Portugal (www.youtube.com/c/ExpatsPortugal) - A channel featuring videos on living, working, and retiring in Portugal, shared by expats residing in the country.

Portuguese With Carla (www.youtube.com/c/PortugueseWithCarla) - A language-learning channel focused on teaching Portuguese language and culture through engaging videos and tutorials.

Portugal Property Guides (www.youtube.com/c/PortugalPropertyGuides) - A channel providing insights into the Portuguese property market, offering tips for buying, renting, and investing in real estate.

Lisbon Lux (www.youtube.com/c/LisbonLux) - A channel showcasing the beauty of Lisbon, including travel vlogs, local attractions, and cultural experiences.

Hygge Journey (https://www.youtube.com/c/hyggejourney)

Other useful links

International Tax Consultant
https://wandererswealth.com/

Portuguese/UK Tax Accountants
https://www.fresh-portugal.com/

Tax calculator tool
https://mytaxes.pt/

Traveling with pets from outside the EU
https://www.dgav.pt/vaiviajar/conteudo/animais-de-companhia/transito-internacional/

Property search websites

https://www.idealista.pt/

https://casa.sapo.pt

https://www.imovirtual.com

https://www.remax.pt

https://www.custojusto.pt/lisboa/lisboa/imobiliario

https://www.era.pt/

https://bpiexpressoimobiliario.pt/

https://www.lardocelar.pt/

https://www.portadafrente.com/

https://homelovers.com/

https://rentola.com/

https://supercasa.pt/

https://casa.iol.pt/

https://www.olx.pt/imoveis

https://www.kwportugal.pt/

These websites, resources, and YouTube channels can provide valuable information, tips, and insights for navigating life in Portugal, whether you're a resident, expatriate, or planning to move to the country. Remember to explore and research further to find the most relevant information for your specific needs and interests. I highly recommend looking for expat or immigrant groups on Facebook in your specific area.

11 THE JOURNEY AHEAD

Congratulations! You have reached the final chapter of this guide, and your exciting journey to Portugal awaits. As you embark on this new chapter of your life, we would like to extend our best wishes and provide some parting words of encouragement.

Moving to Portugal offers you the opportunity to immerse yourself in a vibrant culture, explore breathtaking landscapes, and create lasting memories. Whether you're seeking a change of scenery, career opportunities, or a slower pace of life, Portugal has much to offer. It is a country known for its warm hospitality, rich history, and remarkable quality of life.

As you settle into your new home, remember to be patient with the transition process. Moving to a foreign country can be both exhilarating and challenging, but with an open mind and a willingness to adapt, you will find your place in the Portuguese community.

Take the time to explore and embrace the unique cultural aspects and daily rhythms of Portugal. Engage with the locals, learn the language, savor the local cuisine, and participate in the festivals and traditions that make this country so special. By immersing yourself in the Portuguese way of life, you will not only enrich your own experience but also build lasting connections with the people around you.

Throughout your journey, it is important to stay informed and seek guidance when needed. Use the resources, references, and tips provided in this guide to navigate the various aspects of life in Portugal, from visa and residency procedures to finding accommodation, establishing networks, and understanding the local systems.

Remember that this is your unique journey, and everyone's experience will be different. Embrace the challenges, celebrate the successes, and allow yourself to grow and evolve along the way. You have chosen an extraordinary destination, and Portugal welcomes you with open arms.

We wish you all the best as you embark on this new adventure. May your days be filled with joy, discovery, and a deep sense of belonging. May you create cherished memories and find fulfilment in your new life in Portugal.

Boa sorte e seja feliz! (Good luck and be happy!)

ABOUT THIS BOOK

This book is designed to provide information relating to moving to Portugal. It is sold with the understanding that neither Amazon, the publisher or the author is hereby providing legal, immigration, financial, investment or other advice that should be sought from a professional. Whilst best efforts have been used in the creation of this book, it makes no representations, warranties or guarantees to accuracy and completeness and specifically disclaim any such implied warranties. The advice and guidance may not be suitable to your personal circumstances. You are encouraged to do your own research and consult an appropriate professional.

Printed in Great Britain
by Amazon

23720578R00056